To: Debbie and Al
Best Wishes & Love
Anne Leona Diependeek
2018

Still

Broken

A Memoir

Leonora Diepenbeck

iUniverse books may be ordered through booksellers or by contacting:

iUniverse
1663 Liberty Drive
Bloomington, IN 47403
www.iuniverse.com
1-800-Authors (1-800-288-4677)

Any people depicted in stock imagery provided by Thinkstock are models, and such images are being used for illustrative purposes only. Certain stock imagery © Thinkstock.

ISBN: 978-1-5320-3077-2 (sc)
     978-1-5320-3076-5 (hc)
     978-1-5320-3078-9 (e)

Library of Congress Control Number: 2017913027

Print information available on the last page.

iUniverse rev. date: 01/08/2018

My Battle With Post Traumatic Stress Disorder

PTSD

Resulting in Physical, Psychological, Spiritual and Financial Afflictions

Sherry, Carey and Cory

I Love Being your Mom

To Sherry, for your caring, proficiency, grace and your zest for peacefulness.

To Carey, for your caring, unrelenting aptitude and
your perseverance in some challenging times.

To Cory, for your caring, unique intelligence and for your nurturing nature.

Acknowledgments

My sincere gratitude is extended to my children and their supportive partners: Sherry and Stuart, Carey and Tina, Cory and Kelly. Thank you for your caring, support and for persevering with me through some arduous times. I regret your own losses and appreciate the sacrifices made.

Thank you to Carey for your assistance with electronics and to July O'Regan and Casey Martin for your assistance with photo images.

I extend a special tribute to my grandsons, Walker and Carson, for often engaging me in some spontaneous dialogue, for your interest in, and especially for cheering me on with my project.

Although not directly related to the writing of my memoir, I extend accolades to and acknowledge the following:

My appreciation to all who have responded and helped me with my afflictions, medically and otherwise—I am grateful for your professionalism and hard work amidst some difficult encounters.

To the numerous support groups, I extend my gratitude to the efficient staff and interesting participants. The transport services of Disabled Adult Transit Service (DATS) and the Society of Seniors Caring about Seniors (SSCAS) are highly commendable and appreciated. For life enrichment, the START program at Glenrose, the Southside Seniors Program, Art instruction classes, are all exemplary—Thank you for your goodness and inspiration.

To my co-residents where I reside and numerous others, inclusive of many strangers, for assisting me when ambulating is difficult, my heart-felt thank you.

I also extend appreciation to all who have accepted me as I am with all my shortcomings— by socially filling some voids in my life. When my ability to paint diminished, I needed to do more than just write. In addition to time spent with my family I am thankful for being taken to a dance venue occasionally, for some light-hearted conversations with Paddy, for the comradeship with the players and mutual spectators at the sports centers and the birthday celebrations with my friends Victoria, Georgina, Theresa and Lu, are most enjoyable. To my long-time friend Jim, for being so supportive and understanding of my dilemma, for being there through it all, I am most appreciative. You have all helped fill some of that void and you are all special.

Finally, I am prayerfully thankful for my own fortitude and ability to rise above the adversities that frequent me, still. Nonetheless, I look forward to the future positively—and with enthusiasm.

Introduction

This is a most revealing memoir. You will learn to understand some of PTSD's bizarre symptoms as they are for me. "Still Broken" withholds nothing. My life situation is rather unique and I am anxious to portray to you what I know about PTSD.

I was living a fulfilling and rewarding lifestyle when everything changed in a flash when I was struck down by a half-ton truck. I cringed in shock as I didn't know what had happened.

I spent many years living with severe pain, anxiety and loneliness. At times I felt no one cared.

Physical and mental breakdowns caused me to lose my working career within the medical milieu which was so important to me. This was followed by the loss of my husband's and my beautiful country estate and ultimately a total marriage breakdown.

All my set-backs came on gradually from flashbacks related to the accident, usually from hearing sirens, seeing ambulances, or seeing grills of trucks, witnessing negative advertisements, to name a few. I would lurch, fall, walk backwards or sideways, even being required to crawl when I couldn't walk. Seeking justice also failed so that I slowly and sadly began to accept my losses. Every day thereafter presented new and painful challenges. I felt worthless and didn't think I could survive, but I never gave up.

One day, when walking through the woods in our beautiful country estate, when I was able to, I was mesmerized by the explicit beauty of nature. As I was so replenished by nature and had a keen interest in Art, I enrolled in an Art Class. It motivated me and I painted zealously, mostly nature scenes. It helped me heal from trauma, a little, and I didn't have flashbacks when I painted. I created numerous paintings, inclusive of my two versions of the "Tree of Life."

Also on the advisement by some of the best of professionals, I was encouraged to write, which I did. At that time I never realized I would one day be writing my memoir.

At present my PTSD is coupled with a profound hearing loss where at times I cannot hear at all. As well, I still often have set-backs where I cannot walk. I do however still strive to be as independent and functional as possible although at times it is extremely difficult— but I persevere! I feel one must never give up living to one's fullest potential in spite of acquired handicaps or setbacks.

Because of my advanced age and some acquired health issues I do feel that my productive days are waning rapidly, thus I am impelled to tell my story now. If I can help someone understand some of the uniqueness and encumbrances associated with PTSD, as they are for me, it may encourage others to cite their own stories which I would be delighted to read.

PTSD is difficult to diagnose and to treat but it is more prevalent than one can imagine. Many are unknowingly afflicted by it, especially those who have experienced traumatic life threatening experiences, and victims of war crimes, like the military, and others. Yet, it is so widely misunderstood by many and not too often written about. It is imperative to seek help for this affliction at its earliest onset.

I have recently been discharged from the Villa Caritas Hospital, where I've been a patient for five and a half months. I have been struggling with post-traumatic stress disorder (PTSD), agoraphobia, and depression as a result—almost entirely—of a motor vehicle accident. As a consequence of this accident, I sustained significant injuries physically, mentally, and psychologically. I was in perfect health prior to the accident.

Although it is lengthy, I will earnestly tell you my story.

Part 1

Chapter 1

On April 27, 1989, I was walking toward Woodward's department store in West Edmonton Mall. I looked in both directions as I was approaching the roadway, and then I realized I had forgotten in my vehicle the item I'd been planning to exchange at the store. I returned to my vehicle and retrieved the package, and as I approached the store, I felt a strong force go through me; it felt like a building had hit me.

I found myself lying on the ground with a very frightened man holding my hand, apologizing. I asked where I was and what had happened. He said, "You have been hit by a truck, and I am the person that hit you."

I turned and saw the grill of his truck and smelled either gasoline or alcohol. According to a witness, I was thrown onto the hood of his vehicle and then onto the ground. There was a great commotion, including an airplane flying overhead and an ambulance siren.

All these noises are triggers for me now, along with West Edmonton Mall signs, some lawyers' advertisements, grills of trucks, and pictures of trucks in newspapers—in particular their grills.

My life flashed before me, and I thought I wouldn't be seeing my family again. Because of the force with which I had been struck, I thought I would die of internal injuries. My daughter was in England at the time, and my older son was living in British Columbia. Only my younger son was living at home, and my husband was at work.

I was driven by ambulance to the nearby hospital. There was a great deal of commotion— people standing around, someone taking my pulse, an airplane flying overhead, ambulance sirens, as I have previously mentioned.

When I was examined at the hospital, my injuries didn't appear to be serious. There were no broken bones, and the doctor who treated me said I had a soft-tissue injury. I was given a tetanus shot and some analgesics. When I got off the examining table, I had difficulty walking, as my legs, knee, and hip were injured, so a nurse brought a wheelchair. When I arrived at home, I experienced neck pain, headaches, and spasms all over my body—and fear. I took a multitude of analgesics.

This is what transpired after the accident: I was struggling with my health, and I struggled financially later because I lost my job. According to the doctor's diagnosis, I had sustained a brain injury. I developed PTSD, agoraphobia, conversion reaction, ataxia, panic attacks with fear (particularly fear of being alone), nightmares, unrelenting pain and spasms throughout my body, along with bowel and bladder incontinence, infections, insomnia, and tinnitus that almost drove me out of my mind—and did a little. I also had jaw pain when a tooth broke off after the accident, and I developed trigeminal neuralgia.

I had nine or ten hospital admissions related to the above diagnoses, numerous medical appointments, and a multitude of prescribed medications, which no doctor was monitoring at the time. I had an imbalance and mobility problem and required the use of a wheelchair.

Flashbacks of that accident caused me to fall and lurch, and I was often unable to walk at all. I ended up crawling. This still happens now. With these flashbacks, I require the use of a wheelchair, or I need to hang onto furniture to walk, or I crawl. When I'm lucky, I have assistance, but very often I'm on my own.

This accident caused many losses for me, as well as for my family. It ended my working career. Six weeks after the accident, the office manager dismissed me from my job as a medical dicta-transcriptionist. As she worked off-site, she was often unaware of the functions of the office staff. I tried but was unable to perform the functions required because of physical and mental trauma. I took an enormous amount of analgesics, and on my lunch breaks, I rested in my car or on the examining table in the surgical office where I worked.

I was devastated about losing my job. In retrospect, I couldn't and shouldn't have been working. But I didn't think I should be faulted for trying, as I had a strong work ethic and was trying my best. We were badly in need of this second income, and I wanted to work. If I could have, I would have.

I received one month's severance pay and three weeks paid vacation. I felt I was performing my duties as best I could under the circumstances. I loved my job and enjoyed working for the two surgeons, who treated me well. I had come there with very good references from some reputable employers.

I was in that job for five years and earned $30,000 a year working a four-day week. I had experience as a medical secretary and in office management, having worked in the medical milieu for practically my entire working career, never having been unemployed. I had taken courses in anatomy, physiology, and medical terminology while I worked at the Cross Cancer Institute. I had also taken courses in office management and speedwriting at two colleges.

A leading oncologist at the Cross Cancer Institute noted in a reference, "It is difficult to describe the quality of Ms. Diepenbeck, as there is no other word but *excellent*. She can get along with everyone." I loved working for him. He was so dedicated to his profession that he spent his vacation teaching medical students in Karachi, Pakistan. Unfortunately, he succumbed in the waiting room of the Cross and never recovered—he had been determined to see just one more patient. He was totally dedicated, and his loss was and is felt by many.

The surgical office job wasn't the only job I had enjoyed but failed at. I worked as a departmental secretary in another health care institution, and although I was a proficient dicta-typist, I encountered difficulties typing from handwritten drafts. Although plentiful, the dictating equipment was not utilized in that department. I had numerous responsibilities, including answering a twenty-two-line telephone system, where the calls were often unrelated to the functions of that particular department. I also had an uncorrectable auditory impairment; consequently, to get my attention, the head of the department knocked on the wall of our office, which was adjacent to his. He would often arrive for work at noon, making demands.

I became stressed. And I complained, which was my downfall. I tried desperately to be a worthy employee. For example, at my own initiative, I recorded minutes of departmental meetings and transcribed them later at home. It didn't matter; I was called in weekly to review the mistakes I had made. I heard nothing positive, and I'd leave the office in tears. I was also told I would never get another job on campus. I did have some credibility, as I was called by epidemiology to work as their secretary, but I was already happily employed in the surgical office.

This dismissal still has its effects on me. When I travel in that area of the city, I have a flashback.

Then there was the loss of our beautiful country home, which my husband and I had built with some help from our children. The property became quite neglected, inside and out. I could no longer do much, while my husband was busy working, driving me to appointments, and looking after some of my needs. But then I became too much of a burden, and that *failed*.

Nightmares and bad dreams were occurring—and I still have them. I would wake up screaming. I stumbled around and even crawled when I couldn't walk. This still happens when I have flashbacks brought on by sirens, ambulances, grills of trucks, West Edmonton Mall signs, advertisements by a certain law firm (a firm that did me no harm, but triggers in my mind how my own lawyers didn't help me), and sometimes advertisements by the insurance company involved. This PTSD trauma prevails, and I have had almost no treatment to help me overcome these afflictions. My husband and I could never be intimate after the accident, because I was constantly in pain. I was and still am a mess.

I was no longer able to be a proper wife. I wasn't able to keep up with house or yard, and I had no help. I no longer brought home a salary, and we needed both to survive on the acreage. Affection no longer prevailed, and my husband turned to another woman. This terminated our thirty-five-year marriage, which was sacred to me. Although my husband persevered initially after my accident, he subsequently became extremely abusive to me.

Chapter 2

As we were in a desperate financial situation, I finally, reluctantly, consulted with a law firm that specialized in personal injury, only representing the party that was injured. Repeated requests to our lawyers for assistance were in vain. All they did was send me documents, including medical and hospital reports that confirmed some of my diagnoses. They later sent me an affidavit and Amended Statement of Claim, which obviously they paid little heed to. Because of my mental status, I didn't understand the significance of what those documents meant and what I was entitled to.

We were in extreme debt, and our bills escalated due to interest charges. Our Visa bill was almost $15,000, and our bank refused to carry us. Most of our payments to the bank covered only interest charges.

It was so bad, when our laundry appliances broke down, we couldn't afford to replace them. When I was still able to drive but my car broke down, I couldn't afford to have it repaired. Our dog, Lady, helped me; I held onto her collar when I was having trouble walking. When she became ill, we couldn't afford proper veterinarian care for her. We were strapped.

All our lawyers did was ask us to save receipts. This, in itself, was a joke. We couldn't save receipts because we had no money to provide what was required. I borrowed $3,000 from my eighty-three-year-old mother, who was in need of it for her own health care. Our daughter paid most of our bills, which were well over $10,000. I don't believe I ever repaid her or my mother.

Here is another example of one of my many stressful and hurtful situations: When I was referred to a psychology walk-in clinic, I was totally stressed, in pain physically and emotionally, and hadn't been sleeping. I was seen briefly but not counseled. I asked to use their telephone to get a ride home, but I didn't even know whom to call, as my husband was working out of town. I was told to use the pay phone across the hall, though *I couldn't walk!*

On one occasion, while I was still able to drive, shortly after the accident and after our laundry appliances broke down I was driving to the laundromat, and I heard and saw an ambulance. I knew everyone at home was safe, as I had just left there. But I drove back home. My husband was splitting wood, and my daughter, Sherry, was sleeping. (She worked nights at the hospital.) I drove back to the laundromat and filled the washing machines.

I had a very difficult time from then on. I was frightened by sirens, parking lots, pedestrians, vehicles—and I just panicked. I just sobbed. I didn't want to go home and be seen that way, although they had seen me crying a lot. So I went for a long drive on RR 231. I didn't know where I was going.

I found a wooded area with trees and a path. I went partway in and then back out again. I wasn't afraid then. I started to relax, and as I was driving home, I passed my son, Cory. He stopped and reminded me that we were to go to dinner at a friend's place. We did go, and it was a beautifully planned evening. But I didn't feel well, either physically or emotionally, so I contributed little to the evening. On the way home, however, I was desperately frightened by everything: road signs, trucks, trains. I had extreme fear and panic.

Chapter 3

1990 (This is taken from part of my diary, verbatim.)

Early January. Physiotherapy. Today I am upset and depressed re my lack of progress. Cried. Physiotherapist told me to do at least one thing I enjoy each day. After basic necessities and appointments, I have no energy or desire to do anything else. Neck stiff and sore. Bladder urgency, irritability. He suggested I try Aquacize. Poor balance in the water plus bathroom urgency. My body was jerky—I couldn't relax. Always taking two Tylenol 3s. Weird dreams—very restless. Bladder urgency continued; urgency and frequency with pressure and sharp pains. Am having ringing in my ears almost every night. Have had imbalance for a few months. Tingling sensation in back of neck along with buzzing sensation in my head—accompanied by headaches. Was referred to an orthopedic specialist. Wanted to paint but was too tired.

In February I saw an otolaryngologist re ringing in ear, especially when trying to sleep. Had an audiogram. He said ringing was a result of injury to neck. I asked if there was anything I could take. He said to consult with my family doctor. Ringing +++. It drives me crazy when I am trying to sleep. Tylenol 3s. I hate to take Tylenol for ringing but do not know what else to do. Later my bladder urge (spasms?) increased, and there was an extreme pressure to void and a burning sensation. On going to bathroom, nothing to void. Plus headache, sore legs, and continuous ringing (tinnitus). Was referred to a urologist who performed a cystoscopy.

Sometime in March, my whole left arm and hand became numb. Awakened at 2:00 a.m. with very loud ringing +++. It's hopeless. Hissing every night. I can't bear it when I try to sleep. It makes my other problems seem like nothing. The urologist said I need another test next week. What's new? The ringing, hissing, will drive me crazy. Also my bladder urges me constantly; it is a pressure sensation in the pit of my pelvis. It is a sensation of tics and jabs in my stomach too. My lower back hurts with stiffness, as well as my neck and shoulders. Will discuss medications with my family doctor tomorrow. I need something for sleep. I need Tylenol. I've had Aventyl and Elavil. Really depressed on Elavil, and my body was more jerky, especially at night. Discussed medications with my family doctor. At this time, I take Inderol, Aventyl, Os Cal, Librax, Gravol, and Tylenol.

Every night I have ringing. I truly understand why Van Gogh cut off his ear. I understand he was troubled with a ringing problem but had Meniere's, I believe. I actually did an art gallery tour with Vicky but was very tired. I am very upset. I don't have a car or money. I saw another doctor, as my family doctor was away. I totally broke down during this appointment and complained how I am physically and emotionally drained. She was very kind. I took more of her time than I should have. It was decided to increase the Aventyl.

In April, I endured unrelenting bladder urgency but was unable to void—just like when I went to the emergency room at the University Hospital. Neck stiff and sore as well as lower back. Bladder sensation weird—a prickly feeling with pressure. Ringing goes on all the time. I can barely put up with it anymore. Bad dreams all week. (Everyone dislikes me in my dreams and wants to get rid of me.) Did some painting with Vicky, who is so talented, but it was difficult for me.

Easter, went to church with Stevie. Good. Ringing. +++++ Nothing helps. It seems to be getting louder. Legs ache, very difficult to get to sleep. I disturb Ernie. He would like me to find another place to sleep. What to do? I can't live like this. I told my physiotherapist that it is a year since my injury and that I should be recovering by now. He didn't reply. I take a sleeping pill at eleven at night, and I'm up at three-thirty in the morning with a ringing headache, and both legs ache.

One day in April, I awoke feeling rested. No ringing all day. My best day! My bladder kept me busy, but I didn't care. Only someone who has experienced the ringing, which sounds like sh-sh-z-z-z-z, gets it and tries to sleep with it. Only that person can understand the agony! My happiness was to be short-lived as the ringing resumed that night—with a vengeance. I tried everything I could think of. I didn't want to take a sleeping pill and Tylenol. Listened to two tapes, read, drank hot milk. Finally at two-thirty in the morning, sleep came. Of course, I was upset the next morning as the lack of ringing was so short-lived.

I needed groceries but couldn't go because I was tired, irritable, and lacked money. Ernie went to work at a trade show. The yard is a mess. I thought if I'd sit on the ground and work on the plants, I'd be so exhausted I'd sleep. It didn't work. Came in and stiffening up. Took a sleeping pill at eleven, still awake at two in the morning. Took two Tylenol 3s. Still awake at three thirty. It was my worst night! This ringing will drive me crazy, if it hasn't already! Taking sleeping pill and Tylenol every night, or I wouldn't get any rest at all.

May. Have tried working in the yard, mostly sitting on the ground. It helps mentally but is physically tiring. Then I stiffen up and don't get proper sleep anyway. Stiff in the mornings. Hot bath and exercise help to some extent. My note: "Ringing prevents me from getting any sleep at night. I am desperate. Taking medications as advised. Some say there is no cure for tinnitus."

Physiotherapist asked when I was seeing a neurologist. Told me to tell the doctor about concerns I have, not to worry about being a complainer. Said he's written to my family doctor twice. I was concerned about whether the physiotherapist was being paid. My family doctor advised me to discontinue Aventyl, as I'd been on it for a long time.

Mid-May. Regretted not mentioning jaw pain to my family doctor yesterday, as today it has bothered me all day. Worse in evening. Phoned dentist at the University Hospital and was seen that day. Jaw, reddish area. Referred me to another dentist at the same hospital. Was given a prescription. The dentist said taking sulfa for bladder and Erythrocin won't harm, may help. I'm worried. Something is seriously wrong. Went to an appointment with one of the dentists but am not disclosing names at this time.

I was overwhelmed by his professionalism and understanding of what I was experiencing. He had no answers but talked about a dormant virus being activated. He took a culture and gave me an Rx for mouth rinse and Zovirax. I don't remember much of what he said, but I felt confident with him. He ordered more lab work and said to call him next week, or sooner, if I needed to.

Then I got excruciating pain. Left side of face. Sharp pain in jaw. Took all my medication, which helped for a while. Jaw and mouth still sore, back of neck up to skull very painful; I massaged. Ringing continues. Physiotherapy helped some but by the afternoon, neck was going into spasm. Taking Tylenol and sleeping pill every night. Redness of face and neck.

I later learned that I had trigeminal neuralgia. I continued on antibiotics and lost a lot of weight. The dentist said that with the type of injury I sustained, he was referring me to a neuromuscular specialist. I felt confident again. But problems continued.

End of May: Jaw still hurts. Bladder still aches and burns. Am trying desperately to get well, but am suffering physically and emotionally. Can't sleep without a sleeping pill, regardless of how hard I try. Jaw pain comes and goes.

Talked with Liz. She has malignant carcinoma of the breast. Feel bad for her, such a wonderful lady and friend.

The sixteenth of May, I went to the bank and withdrew my last $800 from my RRSP to pay bills. I then bought some bedding plants and some baby geese from a hatchery. Ernie bought me some ducklings—for Mother's Day, I believe. I kept them on a heating pad until they were ready to be taken down to the pond. They are pets. Ernie built a house for them on the pond on our acreage. If I can't be well, maybe I will be happy. Maybe we will all be happy. I am so hard on my family.

Now my hearing in my left ear was very bad. *Is it because of the tinnitus?* I wonder. I used to hear normal conversation around the house, also television. Now I don't, so I'm a nuisance if I ask for the television to be turned up or a statement repeated. Will I end up in psychiatry? I am trying to get well but am physically, emotionally, and mentally drained.

Chapter 4

One day in May 1990, I noted that it was my worst day. My husband and my daughter were taking me to the hospital—one of many admissions related to the accident. I felt I was insane or very, very close to it. My whole body trembled. I was sick physically, mentally, emotionally, and spiritually. I was delirious, and on the way to the hospital, I thought it fell upon me to pray for everyone. I prayed for forgiveness of my sins and those of everyone else. I begged God to teach us how to help each other, to work together, and to pray together. I prayed to our one God to help us all, no matter what our faith. I was delirious and very frightened.

I asked Sherry if I was sick (meaning insane), and she replied, "No, if you were, they would tell you." But I knew I was insane or very close to being there.

At the hospital, I spent all day having various tests. I was very frightened, and only the presence of Sherry and Ernie made me feel safe. I had apparently been on the following medications: Librax, Halcion, Propranalol, Osteoforte, Elavil, Aventyl, Ativan, Zovirax, Probanthin, Tylenol 3, and Chlorhexidine mouth rinse. I spent three sleepless nights on that hospital stay.

My discharge diagnosis was acute delirium secondary to Benzodiazepin withdrawal, acute panic attacks, dependent personality, chronic dysthymia, chronic neck pain, PTSD, tinnitus, left jaw pain (secondary to dental problems), functional ataxia, and migraine headaches. My lawyers gave me this discharge summary; they were good at sending hospital and medical reports but never helped me in any way.

I wasn't totally well when I was discharged. I never took medications that were not prescribed for me. I always followed my doctors' instructions. I didn't drink alcohol. When I found it difficult to drive my car, I relied on family members to drive me.

The lawyers and insurance companies never offered an alternative arrangement for transportation to appointments. I couldn't keep some required appointments, as I couldn't afford a taxi and had no other means of getting there. I lived in the country—removed from the public transportation system. I relied very heavily on family members, mostly Ernie, to take me to appointments. I did attend a pain clinic and numerous support groups, where strangers were required to help me when I fell or couldn't walk.

Chapter 5

On a visit to Stu's and Sherry's country home in May, 2016, my daughter, Sherry, and my grandson, Carson, treated me to a movie, *Miracles from Heaven*. Afterward Sherry drove into a subdivision where Ernie and I once owned a property. She didn't want to do it. I hadn't seen it in years, but so much wanted to. She was concerned it may make me depressed. And it did! I spent the weekend writing, I reminiscing about having lived there, both before and after the accident.

It was a very desirable subdivision in Sherwood Park. Ernie and I had purchased an almost totally treed but scenic acreage in 1979 in Executive Estates, adjoining a twenty-three-acre reserve that was like a park. It was undisturbed, peaceful, and serene. We had no handouts but worked very diligently to make it our dream home. We often worked through the night.

Ernie cleared the land and landscaped it. Horticulture played a huge part for me as well, and I took a landscaping course at Devon in the wintertime, driving there after work. I planted at least thirty-five evergreens. We had two natural ponds, one with pet ducks and geese. Often in the springtime a mallard would join them. I did an oil painting of that pond, as it was one of my favorite places to relax, pray, and meditate. We had outdoor fire pits and created a beautiful rock garden with flowers, shrubs, and a running stream with a waterfall, as well as a fruit and vegetable garden.

We had many wonderful pets, especially our Samoyed, Lady, and two other dogs. This was not by choice, although we loved dogs, the county bylaw's disallowed anyone having more than two dogs. In addition to Lady, we had a too-enthusiastic dachshund named Benji, who one day raced off into the neighborhood fields, likely in pursuit of a rabbit, and never to return. He may have been shot. He was a pleasure to have around, and his death was felt very much, especially by Carey.

Then there was our poodle, Tiffany, whose previous owners had tinted her a shade of mauve. When we were on vacation at our favorite spot in Penticton, BC, we found her lying under our Winnebago, unattended and malnourished; we later named her Tiffany. We provided for her needs—temporarily, we thought. Upon our departure, no one claimed her. We had little choice but to take her with us.

On our trip home, the only place she felt comfortable was at Ernie's feet by the foot pedals. We were harboring her. She was very ill, with a grossly enlarged belly, and mostly slept under the deck. We tried our best to make her comfortable, but she didn't survive for very long. We also had a beautiful white kitten we simply addressed as Kitty.

We missed the departure of these two precious animals, but we still had the joyful and irreplaceable Lady, treasured and loved, especially by Sherry and Cory. She later became a great companion and helper to me. I'm certain everyone who knew her adored her.

I enjoyed feeding the chickadees and other birds, so I would purchase huge amounts of birdseed. Chickadees enjoyed sunflower seeds, and so did blue jays, which were great at emptying the bird feeders overnight. I also enjoyed the presence of the squirrels that frequented the feeders. We were required to work unfailingly on this estate with some help from our children, but it was done with pleasure and with an anticipation of spending our retirement there.

We also did much of the work in drawing up our own house plans, which Ernie subcontracted. We were one of the first inhabitants in that suburb. Ours was a beautiful custom-built home with two see-through stone fireplaces, featuring spacious rooms with abundant windows and patio doors that took full advantage of the expansive views. The wraparound upper balcony and lower decks did too. It was truly our dream home. We enjoyed living there with our children, and it helped make us a strong family unit. Our friends and theirs were always welcome—often enjoying the outdoors and their friendships. We also had visits from other family members, especially my dear mother.

Everything changed after the accident. I loved nature and the outdoors, and although I would find much peace and comfort on the acreage, it was no longer a solace for me. When I ventured outdoors to walk or work in the yard or seek pleasure and comfort from nature and our pets, I could no longer do that. When a vehicle drove by or an airplane flew overhead, I would drop to the ground in fear and panic. I couldn't walk, so the only way I could return to the house was by crawling or walking backward or sideways. Even trying to go to the mailbox was futile. Sometimes my husband, one of our children, or a stranger would have to support me to get me back into the house, often by almost carrying me. This happened repeatedly.

Consequently I soon became housebound and knew I was becoming a burden and an encumbrance, although no one said so at the time. I was fearful of being alone at home and had a multitude of flashbacks/triggers from my accident. I had PTSD, depression, and agoraphobia, which, to me, was a fear of fear. I would disturb my husband at work, begging him to come home. Our children helped when they could, but they had busy lifestyles of their own and jobs they needed to avail themselves to.

My husband certainly had his hardships and suffered his losses. He took a Realtor course and early retirement with a hope of pursuing that career. This failed because he was too busy driving me to appointments and trying to keep up the acreage.

I had also played a large part in the development and functioning of our property but was no longer able to achieve what was required to keep it up. It soon became neglected inside and out, and we couldn't afford to hire help. Because of my inability to work and have an income, we were financially desperate. We couldn't afford to make mortgage payments, so we were losing our home.

We had planned, as I'm sure most parents do, on leaving the estate to our children after our retirement there. I realize it may not be helpful to ruminate on what might have been, but somehow I feel the need to do this. The aforementioned about having lived on the acreage I wrote at Sherry's and her family's home while I spent a weekend there in May 2016.

Family homestead where I spent my childhood years

Me and the lady who saved me from being struck down by a drunk driver

Ernie and Leona on our wedding day, June 2, 1962

Lady and Cory

Our family when younger

Cory, Leona, Sherry, Ernie and Carey

Our family when older

Ernie, Leona, Carey, Sherry and Cory

Our home under construction in Sherwood Park Lady and Cory in foreground

Our completed home in Sherwood Park

Benji and Carey, Lady and Cory

Carey and Cory fishing in Grand Forks, British Columbia

Carey, Sherry and Cory

Sherry and Stuart

Sherry and Stuart's Wedding

Grandsons Carson and Walker

Walker and Carson

Stephanie and Me

Carey, Tina and Jack

Cory and Kelly, Lakeside property in Lac. St. Anne

Walker, Stuart, Sherry, Carson and Leila

Carson in the Production of The Christmas Carol at the Citadel

Carey and Cory

Ernie, Sherry and Me

My Mom Maria's 75th Birthday

A Family Christmas Celebration in the 1980's

My Friend, Jim, at Lac. St. Anne

My Sister, Katrina, and her husband, Michael, in Cadron, Alberta

Me in Arizona in 2009

Ladies in my condo on my 80th Birthday

Some of my Special Friends

Georgina, Victoria and Jim, Leona and Jim, Theresa and Agathe

Myself and Carey upon Carey's survival after he stopped breathing at the age of two

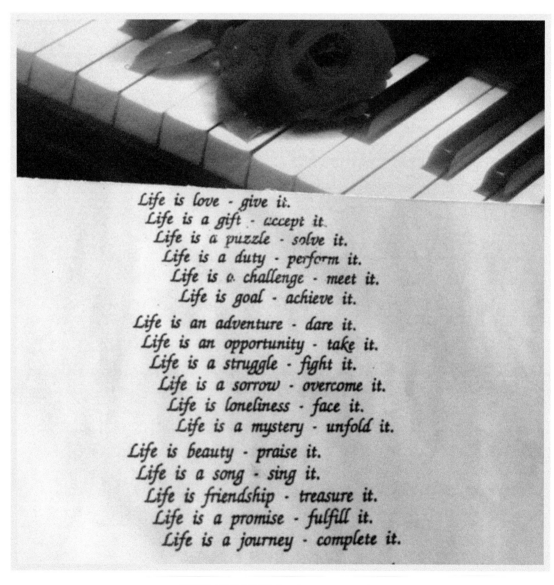

Life is love - give it.
Life is a gift - accept it.
Life is a puzzle - solve it.
Life is a duty - perform it.
Life is a challenge - meet it.
Life is goal - achieve it.

Life is an adventure - dare it.
Life is an opportunity - take it.
Life is a struggle - fight it.
Life is a sorrow - overcome it.
Life is loneliness - face it.
Life is a mystery - unfold it.

Life is beauty - praise it.
Life is a song - sing it.
Life is friendship - treasure it.
Life is a promise - fulfill it.
Life is a journey - complete it.

LIFE IS LOVE Author uncertain

CHEERS

Sherry and me on my 82nd birthday

Chapter 6

I will now look back on 1990. I will try to refrain from identifying specific individuals—medical or otherwise. It is difficult, but all I say is truthful.

I was treated very respectfully at the dental clinic at the University Hospital and was overwhelmed by the understanding of those who treated me. At the time, I felt they were the only ones who cared and understood that I was having difficulties. There it was suggested that I go to the psychology walk-in clinic at the hospital to arrange an appointment, because I wasn't doing well. I did, and an appointment was scheduled for the next day.

When I arrived, I was asked to sit in a corridor. I sat there for about an hour and a half, under extreme stress, as I hadn't slept the night before. On an end table was a magazine with the headline "And Miles to Go Before I Sleep." I felt it applied to me.

I continued my vigil, sitting there, hoping I could lie down and rest, as I felt I would collapse if I didn't get rest soon. While I waited, many people walked to and fro. I recognized some, having worked in the Department of Psychiatry, Division of Psychology, at the University Hospital for three years. No one acknowledged me. I just wanted to disappear, as this ordeal was worse than anything any human being should be forced to endure. Again, I had been very run down and was stressed out from fear and a lack of sleep. I was physically, emotionally, mentally, and I think, spiritually exhausted. Was this normal? Why was I subjected to so much more stress than I had been having already.

The thought of that morning still pains me.

Finally I was called in for a visit with a psychiatrist with two other staff members present. It was a very brief visit at which time I was given a week's supply of Aventyl with instructions to return to my family doctor.

On another occasion, I had an appointment with a therapist at the psychology walk-in clinic. The plan was that when I was through, I would call a taxi to take me to my mother's lodge, as I was now unable to be at home alone.

After the appointment, I asked to use the telephone. The receptionist said there was a pay phone across the hallway that I could use, but I was stressed out and could barely walk. I also realized I didn't have a quarter for the phone.

The cashier's office was to the right, so I stood in line. There were two females acting as cashiers, and each seemed to be involved with something else. My legs were failing me, and I could barely walk. I leaned against a wall. I recall seeing a sign that said "Patient Ombudsman." There was a male attendant in that office, and I was embarrassed because I couldn't hold myself up properly.

Finally a cashier was available. I asked for change, and he replied, "That was simple." I staggered across the lobby to the phone and dialed my mom's phone number.

I then stumbled outside to wait. I needed support, but there wasn't an empty seat outside. I leaned against a pillar. I finally was able to get a ride from DATS service. I told the driver that my mom lived at Pleasant View Place, right north of Southgate. He knew where that was and dropped me off. As I entered the lobby, I realized I was in the wrong building—and I couldn't walk. A woman appeared and helped me, but my body kept being pulled to the left and backward. With difficulty, we finally made it to Mom's lodge. I gratefully spotted Mom, cried, and made a scene, I am sure.

After the trade show where Ernie had been working, he was to pick me up for a visit to my family doctor. I couldn't bear the thought of another trip or appointment. So on the trip to that appointment, I was still very stressed and so I closed my eyes until we got there. When I got out of the car, I couldn't balance myself and could barely walk. Ernie practically carried me up the stairs and asked if he could come into the examining room with me. He was angry at what was happening to me.

I told the doctor I had no instructions regarding medications, wasn't getting any sleep, and was stressed out. She seemed surprised at the way I looked and felt. She said I should be admitted to a hospital, but no prescription or advice regarding medication was given, and I was afraid to take medications independently. I desperately needed the right kind of help but wasn't successful in getting it.

I was becoming extremely fearful and begged Ernie to stay at home with me. Initially I'd get comfort from Lady—our beautiful Samoyed—and our ducks and geese, but soon my fears overpowered their solace. Outside sounds frightened me so that I soon became housebound. When Ernie left for work, I panicked.

I hadn't been driving but knew I had to get help. The telephone didn't seem to be working, so I got into our old Thunderbird and slowly drove down the road and past several vehicles. I drove to a neighbor's house across the road, and when I got out of the car, my legs collapsed. I said I needed help.

He and his wife didn't know what was wrong. They asked if I took pills or drank alcohol. They took me home and practically dragged me into the house. My legs were limp, and I was in a state of panic. They massaged my hands and legs. I had what felt like electric shocks going through my arm. I was lying down, and they asked me to cross my arms. They called Ernie and some other person and spoke of an ambulance. Of course, I was very afraid of ambulances.

Ernie drove me to Emergency at the Royal Alexandra Hospital shortly thereafter, where I was attended to by a physician. My balance was very bad, and I was frightened. I was told to go to see a therapist at the psychology walk-in clinic. There Ernie went in with me and tried to communicate that no one was looking after my medication. I wasn't sleeping. I was totally stressed and needed help *now*. As is known, psychologists can't prescribe medications.

At my last appointment, I had been prescribed a week's supply of Aventyl. The therapist said I could wait until Tuesday to see another psychiatrist. She would talk with my family doctor regarding my medication problem. Honestly I was desperate for help, and I was just running from appointment to appointment. I had received no medication. I believe Ernie left me at my mom's lodge for the afternoon.

In the evening, Ernie took me back to Emergency at the Royal Alexandra Hospital. The trips, including going through Emergency, traumatized me so badly, I couldn't walk to Admitting; I went in a wheelchair. Ernie gave me my health card to present to the receptionist. I looked around and panicked. I got my strength from somewhere, because I grabbed my suitcase, climbed up the ramp, and fell because my legs were giving out.

I was able to get into Ernie's car and said, "I am not being admitted there. I would rather ---!" Ernie was upset and annoyed, and who could blame him? He didn't know what to do, so we went back to Admitting to talk to them. I was thinking of running away and was eyeing a bicycle down the street. I was so out of touch with reality!

When Ernie came back, he said there was no admission there for me. I was glad to go home, but that night was terrible. I hadn't slept a wink and was very panicky. I knew I couldn't go another day without receiving help.

When Ernie left for work, he said he would phone my family doctor and have me admitted. I was exhausted, and when I shut my eyes, I saw lots of red and green circles. A therapist from the walk-in clinic at the University Hospital called, asked me how I was, gave me the suicide number, and told me to call my family doctor.

I wasn't suicidal. I could no longer function *at all*. I phoned my sister-in-law, and she came over.

Chapter 7

On August 1, 1990, Ernie and my sister-in-law were taking me to the Royal Alexandra Hospital again. I was very frightened, especially in Emergency. They took me to the ward, but I was petrified and would not stay. I held onto Alexandra's arm like a baby.

Ernie had to leave for work. My family and staff members all tried, but still I was too afraid to stay until I saw the doctor I was told I would see. Finally, at eight in the evening, the doctor arrived. She seemed nice and took my history (or some of it). I was given some medication, started to relax, and agreed to stay. As soon as she left, I changed my mind. But was so glad I stayed. I received some sleeping medication and finally slept. It was the greatest blessing!

I was then assigned to a specialist in psychiatry. I believe he said I had a phobic anxiety. He recommended reading Claire Weekes's books *Peace from Nervous Suffering* and *Hope and Help for Your Nerves*, which were helpful, but getting sleep was the very best part. I attended all group sessions, and I got weekend passes. The psychiatrist gave me a fair amount of homework, including getting into my car (which was to be my safe place, as I had been injured as a pedestrian), driving to the hospital, then driving home and spending time alone at home.

He prescribed medication (I knew exactly what I was to take and when), talking, and walking on the hospital grounds when I could. And I believe I started improving. He was sympathetic about my accident and job loss and said I would have to talk about it if I intended to improve. I still find that difficult to do. But I felt confident with the psychiatrist. He said most of his patients improved, but he was strict. That was fine with me. I wanted to be and stay well.

Some time during my admission, I received a telephone call from my family doctor's receptionist informing me that the doctor was retiring at the end of August and would no longer see me as her patient nor complete any forms that I may require. She suggested I get someone in Sherwood Park.

I was disturbed by this, as this doctor had treated me since my injury in 1989. I asked whether she could complete any forms that may have been required up until the time she had attended me. The receptionist didn't appear concerned about my situation. I had once seen my family doctor's colleague in this practice, and I asked if she would have me as her patient. And she did.

While at the hospital, I attended numerous group sessions and met with my psychiatrist almost daily. He was very helpful and understanding of my illness. I was admitted on August 1 and discharged on September 7, 1990. My discharge diagnosis was agoraphobia due to PTSD.

Upon returning home, I wasn't doing too bad for a while. I was referred to and joined a panic/anxiety support group in Sherwood Park, dealing with agoraphobia. I had physiotherapy once a week and was trying to do Aquacize once a week. I also enrolled in a two-hour weekly drawing class.

While in the hospital, my tinnitus practically disappeared, and my neck, back, and shoulder pain seemed to be less. My balance problem fluctuated from time to time, and I fell occasionally. I learned that my ataxia was due to my panic disorder. I was also referred for follow-up at a mental health clinic to ensure the gains I had made were sustained. Unfortunately I had no way of getting there and didn't get follow-up, to the best of my recollection.

Shortly thereafter, the tinnitus recurred along with imbalance as well as pain in my neck, shoulders, and lower back. And I became depressed. But attending art class motivated me. I hoped I could paint someday. I was in a bad mood, but I thanked God for my doctor and medications, or I would have had another breakdown, I am sure.

In November 1990, I had an appointment with my psychiatrist. We discussed my personal and financial problems as well. When I came home I fell on some stairs and sprained some leg ligaments. The fall was from imbalance.

Later I saw a neurologist and had a similar visit as with the orthopedic specialist. He asked me to walk in a straight line, and I couldn't. While getting off the examining table, I fell. When I asked about the tinnitus, he said, "There is no cure, as you were told by two others." I asked about my neck, back, and leg pain, and he said it was muscle spasms.

I came home, and later that evening I fell between the family room and kitchen, hurting my left foot—just as I had my right foot the week before. Pain persisted in both legs. I wasn't having good days anymore.

An application for a disability pension to Canada Pension Plan was refused on the basis that a person must have a disability that is both severe and prolonged, and I couldn't be considered disabled according to the Canada Pension Plan Administration. It further stated, "If you do not agree with any decision made you have a right to appeal but it must be in writing and you must appeal within twelve months from the date of receipt of this notice."

As I'm writing this memoir so many years later, I need to state that there was no way I could have appealed this, due to my mental and physical state of health. I was barely functioning, and unfortunately I failed to seek appropriate help. I'm not certain why no one helped me. My health and financial situation affected my lifestyle totally negatively.

I continued to have problems. I had no car or money for taxi fare or anything else. I had no way to get to appointments. I was constantly having problems with imbalance, muscle pain, and tinnitus. My whole body ached, and I was extremely depressed.

In November, my family doctor sent a letter to the law firm I had retained, saying I had sustained a great deal of mental and physical injuries from the accident of April 27, 1989, and due to the severity of my problems, it wasn't possible to comment on my prognosis. A similar letter was sent in October of that year by my psychiatrist. My lawyers gave me copies of these letters and many other documents regarding my injury.

This was explained to me by my psychiatrist: Vological: Car (it was a truck) turned world upside down. Cannot bear to lose house, unable to live without job, home, etc. Can't live this way with limitations—neurotic conflict. Emotional: Irrational, stress. Aware of the above intellectually—but emotions don't go with it.

I wasn't improving. I would be frightened upon hearing a siren. My legs ached. When I forced myself to walk and when I fell, then my whole body ached for hours. After attending a Panic Control Meeting (one of many programs I attended when I could), I went to London Drugs to pick up my prescriptions. I couldn't walk from the pharmacy to the front door, and the store was closing. The staff called my home, and my son, Cory, and a friend picked me up.

This was the last time I went to London Drugs on my own. When I was attending Aquacize, I couldn't walk from the front door to my car. My last time there. Ernie took me to see my alternate family doctor. I told her I was no longer having physiotherapy as the insurance company wouldn't cover it and I couldn't afford it. As I left her office, I fell. Ernie had to help me get to the car, one of many such incidents.

I felt that I never wanted to go out again. It was exhausting, painful, and even embarrassing. I felt like a freak. I walked like a person with cerebral palsy, whom I have sincere empathy for. I didn't understand what I was afflicted with.

In 1991, along with my other health issues, I was having severe tinnitus, wasn't sleeping, and I actually thought I was going out of my mind. In a doctor's office, I picked up a copy of *Reader's Digest* because I saw a headline: "Sound of Silence." That issue featured an article on tinnitus. I was well aware no one could help me, and supposedly there was no cure for it. I wrote to the Tinnitus Association of Canada in Toronto, almost pleading for help, sending it to the attention of the coordinator of the program.

> Please send me any information you may have on tinnitus. For approximately 1 and 1/2 years I have been troubled with it. During the past eight months I have had two hospital admissions precipitated by pain from a pedestrian/ motor vehicle injury, loss of job, sleeplessness, tinnitus and eventually a total physical, emotional and mental breakdown. After my last admission in August/ September I was treated medically and was actually able to sleep. Prior to my admission I was in a state of panic. I am no longer suffering from panic (have had a lot of help in this area), however the tinnitus is recurring and becoming more pronounced and more often. I don't think I could survive another episode as my two previous ones. Please send me any information that might help my tinnitus. I have tried multi recommendations but the tinnitus just persists.

I was fortunate to receive a reply from the coordinator of the program, who sent me voluminous information on tinnitus, including how it is important to have stage 4 sleep and appropriate medication. I couldn't find any such help anywhere else. Having suffered from tinnitus herself, she acknowledged that it could cause extreme stress and sleeplessness.

I have sincere empathy for anyone else afflicted with it. I required a huge amount of medication, which was subsequently prescribed by my psychiatrist. The coordinator of the program was very helpful to me, and we kept in touch for a long while.

Chapter 8

Regarding my employment: In January, I believe it was 1991, my psychiatrist sent the following letter to my lawyers, and they sent me a copy of it.

> Further to my letter addressed to you October 24, 1990, I am in a position to comment on Mrs. Leonora Diepenbeck's employability. At the present time she is wholly and continuously disabled from performing any and every duty pertaining to her occupation or employment. With considerable physical and emotional support from her family she is able to function within the home situation. There's no way however that even her home functioning is even 50% as good as it was before the accident. With the controlled home environment is holding her own but there's no way that she could hold down her previous job or anything like it.

The physiotherapist also sent a four-page letter to the law firm, indicating the treatments that were given and that would be further required as a result of my injury, including medical care. He stated, "She would have a higher chance of developing fibromyositis and premature osteoarthritis affecting cervical, dorsal or lumbar spine."

Regarding transportation: While I was still able to walk from my car to places, I drove myself. But in about February 1991, when my walking was deteriorating, I no longer drove. In any event, I had no car to drive. My family, mostly my husband, initially drove me to all my appointments. Upon checking about the transportation system for the disabled in Sherwood Park, I discovered that the nursing home provided this service. That driver drove me to my first appointment with my psychiatrist.

I was trying to use a walker at the time, but we had great difficulty ambulating the stairway, and he said he couldn't take me with the walker, because it was unsafe. The nursing home terminated this service, saying they could transport only their own residents. I didn't fare well with DATS either; it reminded me of an ambulance.

I eventually purchased a wheelchair with help from Aids for Daily Living, and I used it for all outings. In my house, I could usually walk around well until I had a flashback, was upset, was tired, was just coming in from an outing, or a stranger entered. This varied also.

When I went out of doors, I couldn't walk, regardless of whether I was alone or with my dog, or when other people were around. I totally lost my coordination. Later, my back and neck muscles ached, tinnitus worsened, and I was tired. When I entered another person's home or office, I usually had a problem with imbalance and lack of coordination.

Most of what I note is from my diaries, which my lawyers asked me to keep but paid little heed to. In January 1991, I went to West Edmonton Mall, where the accident occurred. There I staggered badly. On another occasion, Cory and a security man had to carry me to the car, because I couldn't walk.

Once I went to the mailbox with Lady, and I heard a siren and was terrified. It was one of many such incidents, including traffic driving by, especially trucks, frightening me, making me step backward or sideways, or even having to crawl. I would cry and barely make it back to the house. I was very upset, and my body ached.

I knew that if it weren't for the medications, I would have been petrified and calling for help. Lady would help me. Later, when I could, I fed the birds, and I enjoyed wildlife and nature, which gave me some comfort.

In March 1991, I was admitted to the University Hospital in the Department of Medicine/Neurology, with presenting complaints of imbalance, tinnitus, and PTSD. I underwent numerous tests and was seen in consultation, but I had great difficulty walking and fell. Some treated me with respect.

Later, the doctor at the hospital informed me that my tests were normal. He said, "Do you want me to find a tumor or cancer or something?"

I replied, "No, but I can't understand why I can't walk."

Then I asked about the plantar reflux, and he replied it was because I was getting better. He said the brain does some weird things sometimes. I asked about how I would manage at home, and he said, "Do you want to go home, or I could put you in an old folks home."

Then he left. I was fifty-five. I went to my room and cried. "What is going to happen if I can't walk?" I told the doctor and many nurses that my legs, hips, neck, and shoulders ached deeply, and I was having a bad headache.

My husband and the doctor decided to have me transferred to the Royal Alexandra Hospital under the psychiatrist that I had been seeing before. The doctor was with an internist, and he was nicer than he had been; he must have thought about what he'd said the day before.

A few days later, a nurse came in to talk about my condition. She told me that some people fake epilepsy. She talked about depression and said the reason they don't bother with me is because, "If a person is psychiatric, they should be in Psychiatry." It was not a good discussion, and it left me more depressed.

I wondered, *Do they think I'm faking my walking problem?* I had severe tinnitus and was transferred to the Royal Alexandra Hospital on March 22, 1991. My discharge diagnosis was functional gait disorder, PTSD, and left ear deafness.

Chapter 9

On March 22, 1991, I arrived at the Royal Alexandra Hospital and had a restful sleep that night. After breakfast, I did a lot of walking with my wheelchair. Then my legs weakened, my body was in spasm and I was very tired.

Ernie arrived later and told me he had spoken with the doctor at the University Hospital and was told I'd be going to the Royal Alexandra Hospital for behavior modification in relation to my walking. The doctor said I read too much medical stuff that I didn't understand and that a lack of plantar reflex meant nothing.

This upset me a bit because I didn't diagnose myself or pretend to know anything about medicine. Yes, I did do a lot of reading on agoraphobia, and it helped me. Plus, after working for doctors and in hospitals almost my entire working career, it was likely I had learned something about medicine. If anything, I tried to play down my knowledge rather than the opposite.

I told my psychiatrist about my concerns, and he said I would walk because I had a conversion paralysis, which would go away after I get my settlement. He knew we are financially strapped, and I hadn't realized this was the cause of my problem. I thought, *Maybe after I complete this memoir, my problems will disappear. That would be nice, but I really don't expect it.*

I'm writing for therapeutic reasons. It keeps me from being idle. I'm not able to pursue my hobby of painting, I can't leave my residence without anyone being with me, and I need my wheelchair in case I have a flashback and walking fails me.

It may appear that I was confronting an injustice done by those who could and should have helped me. Perhaps I was, but I was truthful. It was important for me to state that so many—especially my family and strangers—had been and were supportive, but I didn't believe anyone had been appropriately compensated.

The next day at Royal Alexandra Hospital, I had another discussion with my psychiatrist, and he tried to explain my problem. In relation to the ataxia, he said they had discussed my problem in conference and suggested we go to Consumer and Corporate Affairs. We could keep our house and one car or file for bankruptcy or remortgage. This I discussed with Ernie, and he planned to remortgage.

I finally called my lawyer. There had been no money or word from the insurance company, as they weren't accepting responsibility. I mentioned us contacting a member of our constituency, and the insurance representative didn't respond. At around that time, I withdrew my last $8,000 from my RRSP to pay some bills.

I continued to struggle with health issues both at the hospital and on my home visits. I was an in-patient at the hospital with weekend passes. I attended assertiveness groups while at the hospital. My psychiatrist told me I would have to talk, but I didn't know where to start. He said to start with the accident. I would also have to write to the person who fired me. I felt it was almost impossible, but I wrote letters, as I was required for therapy. But I never mailed them (though I should have).

I was even required to write one to my lawyers. Apparently, those letters weren't strong enough. (I now feel they should have been for real.) My psychiatrist said he would explain to my lawyers that they were written for therapeutic reasons.

Life changed, and I had changed. I would go home to do housework, but there was nothing to look forward to. Ernie was working at the trade shows. I thought if I could walk to and from the mailbox, I'd ask someone to go to the Glen Allen Art Show with me. I reached the mailbox but couldn't return, so I didn't go to the show. I had a wheelchair, but I kept it in the living room—hating the sight of it. There was always a lot of housework that I had a very difficult time doing, so it was mostly undone. When Ernie took me back to the hospital, I couldn't walk, but just twirled around. He seemed annoyed, and I couldn't blame him.

Back at the hospital, my psychiatrist informed me that a student nurse would be spending time with me in Emergency. (I realize now this was a form of prolonged exposure therapy.) A student nurse and I were to go to the ambulance entrance. It was like reliving my accident again. The noise, the siren, the ambulance, the door closing—it all affected me badly and didn't seem real somehow. I was very frightened, and I cried.

The student nurse took me back to my unit and I couldn't walk. I was upset about not being able to walk and that I kept falling, especially when going to the ambulance entrance as part of my therapy. One psychiatrist said I had PTSD and hysterical conversion.

He was concerned about my gait, because I was likely to hurt myself again. He also said I could ambulate in any way that was appropriate for me. He said that I was truly traumatized psychologically at the accident scene and that I may have to live with some of my problems, such as tinnitus and walking difficulties.

While at the hospital, I talked with many patients who were intelligent and interesting. Some of them were practically walking on the ceiling, they were so high. Some were so low, they talked about suicide. They were very kind, often helping me by pushing my wheelchair. Most of these patients needed nurture; some had been discarded and neglected by loved ones. But all I could do, as a patient, was listen and try to comfort them. I realized the challenges the staff must have, especially if they worked there because they cared.

The new patient in our room was frantic. She had been frightened right out of her wits since arriving, and all she did was cry. No one could help her. Another patient was very upset and needed nurturing; her parents were taking her home. She gave me a plant because she said I was good to her. I hope I was and wished I could help her in some way. She wanted her boyfriend back, but he didn't love her anymore.

My regular psychiatrist wanted me to attend groups four times a week after I was discharged. I wasn't sure what group I would fit into. And how was I supposed to get there? I should have attended while I was in the hospital.

Then I met with my psychiatrist and a student intern. I was given a drug prescription, my antidepressants were increased, and I was given a prescription for an Able Walker. My psychiatrist said he would be seeing me on a regular basis.

I couldn't get my meds, as they were locked up, and someone would have to go back for them the next day. I asked about driving a car because of the meds I was on. The psychiatrist said, "I can drive."

The student intern said, "This wimp will call the insurance company and ask if she can drive."

I stated, "That's a nice picture you paint of me."

The therapeutic letter to my former employer was brought up again and was still an issue. I was told that if I didn't send one, I was guilty of something. (Can you believe it?) I think the reason I didn't send it was because I was afraid of being hurt again, but how I wish I had been strong enough to have sent it..

There was no resolution regarding the tinnitus and walking. And that was the end of my stay at the Royal Alexandra Hospital. I was discharged on May 31, 1991.

My discharge diagnosis was PTSD, conversion reaction with ataxia, and imbalance.

Chapter 10

In June 1991, I was home, and it was nice to be home. My sister-in-law, Alexandra, called and asked if we should go out, get some plants, and plant some flowers. We decided to first drop off my prescriptions at London Drugs, but I could barely walk, even with her support and a cane. We then went to Home Surgical, and I purchased the Able Walker on a Visa card. Then at Salisbury Greenhouse I got seventeen dollars worth of plants, which Alexandra insisted on paying for. That was nice of her. I came home tired, and Ernie was at a trade show. Alexandra and I made pancakes, because there was no food in the house.

The next day, June 2, was our twenty-ninth wedding anniversary. The house needed cleaning, and laundry was piled up. I tried to clean while Ernie made dinner. Alexandra came over. The next day, Sherry called and asked if I wanted her to take me to buy groceries. I had no money, so I borrowed from Sherry. She brought over some geraniums and planted them, which was thoughtful of her.

I was very tired all the time and depressed. I had no motivation. I was picked up by the nursing home bus and taken to the Royal Alexandra Hospital Group Meeting one morning. The walker I'd purchased wasn't helpful except for resting at the top of stairs. I had a long interview, going through my history again. It was the same as others, except I was asked who my lawyer was and if I was suing for wrongful dismissal. (I realize now I should have but hadn't a clue how to go about it.) I said I was suing the insurance company of the driver who hit me.

She asked about our marriage, and I said, "It has changed." I further stated, "After all the meds I take, I snore at night, and my husband and I sort of battle all night, with him pushing me to one side so I don't snore." The interview was over, and my ride arrived. It was awkward getting both up and down stairs, and I was stressed.

Ernie was in Calgary. I was happy when Cory was at home most days; otherwise, I might have been afraid again. When I went to feed the ducks on the pond and to pick up the *Journal*, I had a terrible time walking, even with the cane and with the help of Lady.

Later in June, I received a call from the driver from the nursing home, saying he could no longer take me to the group meeting because of the stairs. I'd had a lot of trouble the week before. I called someone at the group and was told if I couldn't get there to attend groups, there was no point in continuing an interview, so it was canceled.

I tried to understand the driver's position. He said that if he dropped me, they would be at fault if I got hurt and could be sued. (I had and have no intention of suing anyone who tries to help me, and I have always express appreciation for the assistance I receive.)

I tried to paint with Vicky but couldn't seem to do it, as I was usually too tired and had headaches. I'd only driven once since being discharged from the hospital. Also, I didn't have a car. Ernie would drop me off on his way to work and pick me up later, if I could go to Vicky's.

I was also upset about being overweight. There was almost no food in the house, no fruit or vegetables, so I ended up eating junk food. I tried on everything I owned, but nothing fit. I needed to lose twenty pounds, but I was always hungry. Maybe it was the meds.

I talked with my psychiatrist, and we went over my meds. Apparently I did receive some money from CPP, but it only covered the Visa payments. Sherry and Mom still waited to be paid back.

June 27: In the week since my discharge, my walking had gone from very good to very bad. At times, I went right down on my knees. The tinnitus was the same. When walking was worse, tinnitus was worse. I required a lot of sleep and was gaining weight. It was very discouraging. Oh, and I fell in the duck pond trying to shut the door to their enclosure. Got soaked.

One day my walking in the house wasn't too bad, so I thought I would try walking along the front driveway. Ernie had just mowed the lawn and told me not to think about anything, but just walk. Well, I tried, and at the same time a neighbor was taking her kids for a stroll. We exchanged greetings, a vehicle drove by, and I was walking backward, sideways—you name it. I got to the entry and sat on a low post and cried.

Just then, Cory and a friend drove up and asked me to get into the car. They drove me to the house, and when I got out, I couldn't walk. My body was being pulled backward. Both boys dragged me into the house. I lay on the floor, exhausted.

In July, I had a long visit with my former family doctor, whom I hadn't seen in a year. She felt bad about all I had gone through. She told me the reason the University Hospital discharged me so quickly was because they didn't want me to think of the place as an institution. She said it made her dislike their attitude. It also made me feel very upset. I couldn't believe they didn't understand that I was having problems and just couldn't help myself to get well. She said she would continue to be my doctor and would do a complete medical in the fall. We talked about physiotherapy and where to go, as I had no transportation. I was going to try to go back to my original physiotherapist, as the office was near Ernie's office, and hopefully he could drive me. I'd had about five incidents of incontinence in bed but hadn't told my former family doctor.

July 13: I slept in our bedroom. When I awoke early, I had wet the bed. Ernie was gone, and I thought it was a workday. When I came downstairs, I found him sleeping in the family room. I commented on it, he said, "How can I sleep with someone who snores and now wets the bed."

I was sad for both of us. I didn't think Ernie cared anymore, and who could blame him. He asked what I'd do. I said, "I'd probably be concerned as to why it's happening." The bedwetting kept on occurring, so I was washing all the bedding time and time again. Maybe this wasn't a big issue, but I wondered why it was happening.

Ernie came home one day and said he had seen a doctor because of chest pain. The radiologist had taken x-rays and something had shown up on one lung. The doctor was treating Ernie for pleurisy but thought it could be pneumonia, a collapsed lung, or something else. We were all upset and concerned. Ernie thought it was a nerve problem. He later had thirty-two x-rays and was informed that there was a splattering of lung cancer, but it was not the primary site of the cancer. An ultrasound of his abdomen determined it was the primary site.

This was devastating. Ernie has done so much for all of us and was now struck with cancer. I hoped and prayed that he could be helped. I wouldn't want to go on if anything happened to him. He was everything to me—husband, father of our children, friend, mentor, always doing for others. He was acting very strong and brave—more than I had been able to do.

The basement needed cleaning, flowers needed watering and weeding, and I couldn't walk anywhere in the yard, so I hated going outside. I was going to try to walk to the mailbox one more time. I couldn't; I crawled back to the house.

I had a call from my lawyer asking if they could photograph me walking outside. I said, "Yes, but I would prefer not to know when, as I am worse if someone is watching me." She said she didn't know why I wasn't receiving the $11,000 owed to me. She also stated she would refer me to a neuropsychologist, which she did. She later gave me a copy of his medical report.

On the last day in July, I called my lawyer's secretary because the lawyer wasn't available. I told her I needed a wheelchair, physiotherapy, transportation, and money. I said I couldn't depend on Ernie for everything, as he had health issues and may require surgery. The secretary advised me to phone my psychiatrist. I did, but my call wasn't returned. The lawyer's secretary said the lawyer would call me when she had news for me.

I also called Aids for Daily Living and was informed I could borrow a wheelchair. I had borrowed one from another source before. I also called my physiotherapist and was told they had a referral for me. I responded that I had no way of getting there, but was working on it. I later went for physiotherapy and was asked to sign a form accepting full liability, after Health Care ran out.

In early August, Ernie brought a check from my lawyers. It was for $8,000 instead of $11,000. I called my lawyer, and she stated the insurance company would send the difference of $2,600 soon. The lawyer for the insurance company said to pay it—against his better judgment. Later Ernie took me to see my lawyer, and I received $2,600 and was asked to sign a release from Section B. I required the wheelchair to ambulate.

I continued to have medical problems. I lurched, and my back, head, neck, and legs ached, and I had almost nonstop tinnitus. I took multitudes of analgesics for pain. Later I received a placard for disabled parking, authorized by my psychiatrist. He prepared a letter to Aids for Daily Living about a wheelchair.

I also told my psychiatrist I wanted to take painting lessons but was always too tired. Ernie took me to Vicky's to paint several times, but I didn't do good work. So much needed to be done in the house, and I was always so tired.

One day we had a barbecue down at the fire pit, which my mother and brother attended. I couldn't walk the incline, so Cory had to take me up by carrying the wheelchair with me in it as he couldn't push it uphill with me in it. I state this because I realized I was a problem for everyone, but they didn't complain. Ernie said my outdoor walking had worsened.

Ernie got some test results and was told both lesions in his lungs had decreased because of the medication, Erythrocin. There would be no surgery unless there was a change. I was relieved and know he was as well. Ernie was preparing to go fishing, and I was glad he as finally getting a break. I would do my best, as I would be at home, mostly on my own.

Later that weekend, Carey came and spent the night. I didn't hear him come in but was glad he was so thoughtful. He said something gave him the feeling that he should come home.

September 1: For me, it was a very bad day. I had great intentions of working on my albums or painting, but I thought I would feed the ducks and go for the newspaper first. Feeding the ducks wasn't too bad, but bad enough. Lady helped me. Then I went for the newspaper, but it would be the last time. I just couldn't walk, and it was so hard on my body. I ached for hours.

I was close to the house, resting on the lawn, when Cory and Debi drove up. I tried to get in on my own but had no strength left in my legs. They helped me into the house, and I lay on the floor and cried (one of so many times). Debi said that if I wasn't walking by the time she completed her education, she would help me.

I lay on the Chesterfield, took two Tylenols, and tried to sleep. My whole body ached, and the tinnitus was very bad. I had accomplished nothing and was mostly tired, depressed, and lonely. I knew I wouldn't feed the ducks that night, because I couldn't go through another session of torturing my body.

Earlier Carey had called from the lake to see if I was okay. I tried to diet, but because of depression I filled myself with junk food, mostly peanut butter and jam sandwiches, as there wasn't much else to eat. Then I hated myself for doing it. I knew I should feed the ducks and geese; they and Lady kept me going.

Ernie was away most of the time, so I was often alone.

Chapter 11

September 9, 1991: I had an appointment with a neuropsychologist. In his letter of October 18 to the lawyers I'd retained, he summarized the following in a thirteen-page report.

> Following your request of August 9, 1991, I have had the opportunity to assess your client on September 9 and September 18. I have also had the advantage of reviewing the medical information including your letter of August 9, 1991, and the hospital records concerning Mrs. Diepenbeck's hospitalization between March 11 and March 22.

He summarized it as follows:

> Whatever diagnosis is agreed upon for litigation procedures it should be recognized that Mrs. Diepenbeck is severely debilitated as a result of this accident. She certainly cannot function as she did pre-accident and there is no question that she continues to experience emotional distress, physical discomfort, financial problems and a severely altered lifestyle. If I can further assist you with this case please let me know.

I did attend physiotherapy and was happy to have some transportation, although I heard it was only temporary. It was a Handi Bus, I believe. I asked Ernie if he would take me to a famous singer's performance at the Jubilee Auditorium. He said, "If you can walk, I will." Of course, I didn't go.

In September, we celebrated Sherry's birthday. Attending were Carey, Dawn, Cory (Debi couldn't make it), Kaye, and Mike. Stu also came, bringing a cake and an answering machine for Sherry. We had some happy times. I loved my family, and they meant everything to me and still do.

I was scheduled to have a hair appointment at Bev Facey School one day. I didn't know how I would get there, but I thought I'd have Ernie drop me off and pick me up, or I would try to do it on my own. The car was at home, so I took the foot supports off the wheelchair and tried to get it into the trunk of the car. I couldn't lift it. I then thought I would drive there and enter with the help of my cane for support, although I had my doubts. It was the first time I had driven in a long time.

I parked the car close by and tried to walk. I couldn't do more than two steps before I lurched, twisted, and went in every direction. I got back into the car, and it finally struck me just how dependent I was on others to get me to places. I cried (what's new?) and again felt like someone was drilling a hole right through my heart. I couldn't make it.

Later, at bedtime, Ernie asked who was taking me to my appointment for my perm. I said I thought he would, as I had no other way. He refused, indicating he knew too many people and was upset at having to resort to that type of service (meaning, I guess, having to resort to going to a school for a perm). The next day I called a taxi service and was told they wouldn't take anyone in a wheelchair. I resorted to asking Cory's friend to transport me to and from my appointment, which she did. I hated to be such a bother to others and to be so dependent.

On September 23, I met with my psychiatrist. I indicated I was sad, depressed, and couldn't understand my walking difficulties. He mentioned hypnosis, and I said, "I would agree, but I feel apprehensive about it." I told him I was concerned about Ernie's and my relationship. Nothing seemed meaningful anymore, except sleep, when I could get it.

My psychiatrist was surprised that I'd never had happy dreams. Sometimes I felt that no one cared. I tried to clean the house, but upstairs had become a disaster, and I had no energy. The dishwasher had been broken for months, and we couldn't afford a new one.

I had a driver from the nursing home (I believe it was) drive me to some of my appointments, many of which were continuously cancelled. I thought I would walk on our deck, but couldn't. Lots of airplanes flew low, frightening me, and I took a bad fall. This added to my lack of coordination, and I was continuously falling. A few days later, three people came over to see how I walked outside—and I fell!

My psychiatrist thought I should paint one hour each day. I didn't usually have the time or energy, but I said I would force myself. Ernie suggested I try to do some painting outside.

I tried walking with my wheelchair, but that didn't work. I became upset, cried, and laid in the bushes beside our acreage pond. Ernie finally brought me back in the wheelchair.

I sketched the pond and then tried painting outside on another day. It actually wasn't too bad, so I decided to try again. And I did get to attend Nana Mouskouri's performance on October 15. Love songs are my favorite, and she sang "Only Love."

Ernie was in Calgary, and I was concerned about the ducks. I went down to feed them and thought I would bring them some hay. A van drove by very slowly, and I panicked, walked backward, and fell into the snow. Lady was with me. I cried, and she comforted me. They needed more hay, and perhaps because of attending the show the night before, I was walking better. I fed the ducks that evening.

October 21: I was depressed. I tried to paint all day then wiped everything off. I was never satisfied with my painting skills. I realized later that I was doing abstract paintings and unfortunately destroyed them because they weren't realistic.

Ernie drove me to Vicky's to paint. She worked on her eagle while I tried to do a background for a dog picture. Later I did a painting of Lady, which Carey has; a painting of Cory's dog, Sammy, which he has; and a painting entitled "Tree of Life," which Sherry has. But the middle part of that painting, meaning the middle years of one's life, is dark and perhaps too sad. I also created another version of the "Tree of Life." I loved going to art galleries when I could, but I hadn't been to one in years.

I had a keen interest in art and had focused on some talented artists in the media and in some art galleries. Art was very therapeutic for me; it inspired me and partially helped me heal from trauma. The love of nature and the support of my family enabled me to create numerous paintings. Only a few related to my subject matter, meaning my version of *the tree of life*.

Chapter 12

November 2, 1991: Sherry came over, and with my wheelchair she took me to Kingsway Garden Mall. I really enjoyed myself. She was patient and let me stop and look at things. We went to Photo-Print Poster Shop, where I saw a print of a black-and-white tree, which I really liked. Sherry looked at prints while I wheeled myself to the corner of the store and tried to see if I could walk. I couldn't. A sales clerk came by and asked if I needed some help, so that put me back in my wheelchair.

Sherry and I then had a Cinnabon (full of calories). She purchased a sweater and a blazer. I felt good, almost as if I were walking. It must have been difficult for Sherry.

We came home, and she rented some movies. I watched the first movie and slept through the second one. Sherry slept over. Stu was in Calgary.

In November, I had a call from my family doctor to inform me of an abnormal WBC. She arranged for another WBC test in a month. I relayed my continuous problems with my legs aching, walking difficulties, and new bruises above my knee. I was later given my lab results, which showed low WBC (white blood cell count) and lymphocytes. A back x-ray showed osteoarthritis. She said I should see her again in a month's time and have lab work repeated.

In November 1991, I had a call from Alexandra informing me that my brother, William (Bill), was very ill and that the minister had been called to administer last rites. When we arrived at the nursing home, it was very distressing. He was sitting in a bed on plastic with no sheet under him. The male nurse was feeding him some ground beef, carrots, potatoes, and large chunks of orange with the membrane still on. We were shocked to see him looking so ill, propped up in his chair with no head support.

Shortly thereafter, the charge nurse came in and said, "He shouldn't be eating." Really, we knew that. Next Bill's daughter, Adelle, and the male nurse were on the phone, and Adelle inquired about Bill's medical status. The nurse said Bill was just fine—no problem, lah-dee-dah. My sister, Stephanie, whom we called Stevie, was standing right there and asked to speak with Adelle. She took the phone and said, "No, your dad is not just fine. He is very ill."

We all realized that Bill required more intensive care, but the nursing home staff and whoever else was responsible did nothing, it appeared. Later that evening, we were informed that Bill had been transferred to the University Hospital, and we were relieved. Sometimes it pays to speak out.

On November 12, my psychiatrist sent a letter to my lawyers suggesting hypnotherapy. My lawyers gave me a copy of it. I received a letter dated November 13 from Alberta Aids to Daily Living, informing me that the wheelchair had been approved at a total cost of $1,524.39, which they paid a large portion of. I paid $381.10 on November 27, 1991.

On December 3, I had a bad feeling about Bill. I sent him a rose. On December 6, he was pronounced dead. What sorrow and what heartbreak. He wanted so much to live and had so much to live for. He was intelligent, an educator who earned his degree mostly through summer classes, a philosopher, a musician who played in the Junior Symphony Orchestra, a music teacher who sang in the church choir, and a lifeguard. He was a highly moral person with great love for his wife and children. His wife lovingly stood by him through his twelve years of illness.

I had deep regrets. Why did we not encourage Bill to have the mitral valve replacement twelve years ago? My father, who had built Bill's first violin, was stricken with a coronary thrombosis and passed at the age of forty-eight. (We are so fortunate in that we have so much advancement in medical science now, especially the efforts of the Mazankowski Alberta Heart Institute. I just felt the need to acknowledge that.)

This started out as a memoir regarding my PTSD and its afflictions, but sometimes I get sidetracked, so please bear with me as I express myself partly in the present tense. It's apparent that I write in both the past and the present tense. It's the best way I know how to portray a part of my story.

I realize this is a boringly comprehensive and self-centered documentary of events. Undoubtedly, reminiscing about the past doesn't serve the best interests of myself or anyone else. But somehow I feel the need to do this as my memory is clearer now and I am able to do it, with the hope that I will be able to continue. It takes away from my idleness, as previously stated, due to my inability to pursue what is important to me, such as painting.

I did my last painting in 2013. It sustained the endorphins in my brain, which keeps me functional. I'm also a great lover of music, especially the lyrics—and, in particular, the love songs—by Bryan Adams, which helped me when I had a flashback and couldn't walk. I was and still am a great fan of his, and with some assistance, I created an oil portrait of him. I have no idea what I will do with it or my other artwork. I met Bryan Adams in person in 2000 at Chapters, when he autographed his *The Best of Me* CD, and I have enjoyed many of his performances. One of my favorite songs is "When You Love Someone." I believe he is a musical genius. I am a forever fan of his music and that of all the talented artists.

Also on the bright side, as music is so therapeutic for me, I am now entranced by heart-rending compilations by some of the best, along with Bryan Adams and Nana Mouskouri. Due to my auditory deficiencies, I haven't always been able to hear and enjoy the wonderful sounds of music. To me, some melodic magnificence is portrayed by the following: Richard Clayderman's "Love Story," Adrianni Marradi's "And I Love You So," Andre Rieu's "My Way," plus ABBA, Georgia Zamfir, Lionel Ritchie, Julio Ignasias, Leo Rajas, Susan Boyle, Eric Clapton, Simon and Garfunkel, Sarah Brightman, James Last, Tim Janis, "The Prayer" by Celine Dion and Andrea Bocelli, and Andreea Petcu's videos—to name just a few. For total relaxation, I choose Celtic relaxation music.

Speaking of fans, I am also taken by the acting skills of Robert Redford in *The Horse Whisperer*. I thoroughly enjoyed that movie and have watched it many times. It filled my time and decreased my loneliness. But I was saddened by the injuries in the movie, especially that of the horse. In a way, the suffering of the horse reminded me of when I lived in the country as a child and my dad sold a pet horse for financial reasons to a neighbor a considerable distance away, across a river. Months later, the horse returned to our homestead after swimming the river. It was emaciated and perished in our front yard. So sad!

Although I'm making great progress, I still have many incidents of falling and crawling because of a flashback, even if it's not visual but mentally induced by something related to the accident. This often happens, even when just talking about it, which I refrained from doing for many years. I later heard from some of the highest authorities treating PTSD about the beneficial effects of talking and writing. (Little did I realize at the time that one day I would be writing my memoir.)

I don't profess to be a qualified writer. I have no fancy degrees, my terminology and storytelling is simplistic, and at times I'm repetitive due to some memory loss. The dates of events and some interactions may sometimes be inaccurate, but generally what I state is factual. I try not to refer to specific individuals I have been involved with since my injury, which is extremely difficult to accomplish, as many have been helpful and still are.

As formerly stated, I'm writing this for therapeutic reasons at this time (although doing it can be quite stressful). I can't leave my residence without someone being with me as well as taking my wheelchair with me, for fear of a flashback causing me to be unable to walk.

I hope also that readers realize that others struggle with PTSD and some of the bizarre symptoms associated with it. In all that I've learned about PTSD, I'm not aware of anyone else who has had the symptoms of lurching, falling, walking backward, and having to crawl after flashbacks/triggers related to a traumatizing incident. I don't know if my situation is unique, and I hesitate to bring attention to it or be self-pitying. I write about it in the hope that in the near future, medical science will find an explanation and even a cure for this unfortunate affliction. We still have so much to learn about PTSD.

Chapter 13

1992: As my hearing was also a problem, Sherry took me to an audiology clinic in January to have a mold made for a hearing aid. *Will it make my tinnitus more pronounced?* I wondered. *Should I proceed with the order when I am financially more able to afford it?*

In January, my psychiatrist and I discussed meds, and the Aventyl was increased. We also talked about hypnosis. I couldn't walk, and my limbs hurt. The tinnitus was unrelenting. I don't want to relive past experiences; I just wanted to be able to sleep. It all felt hopeless. As a last resort, I prayed to God for help, and I met with my lawyer and was given documentations, but nothing else.

In March, my psychiatrist and I talked again. There wasn't much change from my usual problems. I couldn't do all the housework properly; vacuuming didn't get done, and the windows, ovens, and all needed cleaning. It wasn't pleasant to live in a messy house.

I had periods when I was very sensitive and was hurt easily. I cried often, and it was worse when the nice weather arrived. My few friends said I didn't call, but I called or tried to call when I wasn't feeling low, as I didn't want to upset others. Plus, my auditory problem made communicating difficult. I tried to paint and thought I would try to take more lessons, and maybe even go to Red Deer College for four days in the summertime. I would have loved to feel well and have a holiday.

Later I saw my psychiatrist. I was very upset and crying about not being able to walk outside. I told him I went the day before to see my winter flower garden and couldn't walk at all, and I fell. He wanted me to see a hypnotist, though he hadn't at first. He wanted me to arrange it on my own or through my lawyers. He said it was about seventy dollars for a one-hour session.

I took an enormous amount of medication, and I couldn't sleep. The doctor's recommendation was for me to write my dreams down. I had a very bad dream involving my lawyers. I didn't want to dwell on things I had forgotten.

I called my lawyer about hypnotism, but she was in a meeting, so I left my telephone number. I then called Psychology Association and Hypnotism in Sherwood Park. The person I spoke with about hypnotism knew nothing about conversion reaction. I thought I would rather go with a medical doctor. Later, the lawyers scheduled an appointment for me with the hypnotherapist.

The tinnitus was constant all day. My back still ached from a fall. I went out again to try to feed the birds. It was an awful experience, as my legs couldn't support me or cooperate with what I was trying to do. Everything seemed so hopeless. If I got tinnitus and couldn't sleep and then couldn't walk (it also happened indoors), what was the use of trying. I just didn't want to get all stressed again. I prayed to God to please help me. Perhaps I spent too much time in prayer—but that was truly what sustained me in my times of weakness.

On April 21 and 22, 1992, I was involved in an Examination for Discovery in which the defendant's lawyer examined me. The defendant also underwent an Examination for Discovery on April 21. I had to respond to sixty-eight undertakings, including providing a list of special damages; of the loss of income, past and future; and of the cost of care, past and future. These undertakings exhausted me, and the lawyer didn't appear to care how I'd suffered from the accident. I stressed to the defendant's lawyer that I wouldn't know how to do this, to which he replied, "Your lawyer will know what to do."

The defendant had only three undertakings at the request of my lawyers: "advise of the last time taking Prednisone prior to the April 27, 1989, accident and the next time thereafter; advise of the date the medical condition was added to your driver's license; and, if requested, provide information from each of your treating physicians, optometrists, ophthalmologists, or neurologists with respect to the optic neuritis." (It's questionable that all or any of the undertakings requested of the defendant were investigated or mattered, though it would certainly appear they had some effect on his driving ability at the time of the accident.)

Chapter 14

On April 25, 1992, I had an introduction to my first of many sessions with the psychologist involved in my hypnotherapy. He appeared understanding, kind, and professional. We had a lengthy history taking, for the ?? time for me with other professionals who had interviewed me since the accident. That's all right, but sometimes I make mistakes on dates and even trivial items.

He made me a tape while I was in a trance. I was really relaxing, except my neck bothered me, and I needed to go to the restroom, which was upstairs. Since I couldn't do stairs, I persevered.

Ernie had gotten me to this office through a window on my first visit there, on a Saturday. I left with a good feeling. We talked about my wanting to walk, and I indicated my tinnitus had lessened a little. I was also able to sleep with medication. I also told the psychologist that I had been trying to get off most of the sleep medication, but it was difficult because the tinnitus recurred.

I listened to the tape faithfully. It hadn't changed my walking yet, but I found it to be relaxing. I'd had a couple of bad days that week, but that was nothing new.

Later Sherry took me to the audiology clinic, and I got my hearing aid. I came home and found that all noises were very pronounced—doors slamming, papers shuffling, dishes being washed—but I was determined I would give it a good try. Well, I'd had practically nonstop tinnitus, and the aid whistled and exaggerated sounds I didn't want to hear. I wore it all day, but by evening I couldn't bear it any longer. The tinnitus was so annoying I had no recourse, so I took all my meds and retired for the night.

The next session with my psychologist (who I will now refer to as my hypnotherapist) wasn't good. I listened very keenly, but the tinnitus was interfering. In spite of my tinnitus, the subsequent visits with my hypnotherapist were quite good, although often stressful when I would go into a trance and relive the accident.

After breakfast on May 9, I read the newspaper. On the front page was a vivid picture of a blue truck with a large grill, a caterpillar, dirt, etc. It frightened me so badly, I couldn't walk. I wanted to put it down or throw it away, but I didn't know how. I wanted it to disappear completely, though I knew it was only a picture. I think that after my accident I turned my head and saw the grill of the truck after I asked what had happened.

I threw that section of the paper and another section following it into an old cardboard box. I still couldn't walk very well and was very upset. I knew I had the chance to conquer this, but how? If I tore it up, if I threw it in the fireplace, if I threw it in the garbage—would that free me? I told Ernie about it, and he told me to get rid of it in my mind. *But I couldn't!*

I thought I could throw it into a river or ocean. But I couldn't, because I love rivers and oceans, and I would be reminded every time I saw one. I thought of sending it to the furthest place on earth, where I'd never go, perhaps Tasmania. This overwhelmed me. I continued with my day, and later (twice), I summoned my courage to peek at it again. Same thing: it affected my walking immediately.

After the third episode, I lay on the floor and bawled. Cory and Debi were over, and I knew it must be upsetting to them, but I couldn't help myself. I called on Stevie to be my advocate, to advise me. She said to just "throw it away with the wind." Sounds easy, doesn't it?

Later that month, I was reading the transcript. It was difficult reading and reliving, and there were errors. I just didn't know how to go through 264 pages and make corrections. I wished that part was over with.

On May 23, Ernie drove me to my appointment with the hypnotherapist. I was put into a sort of trance, where I relived my injury. (He called it my "incident.") I endured two and a half hours of very exhausting work.

We went to the Bay in Southgate Mall to pick up a clock I had purchased for my godchild, and we were required to go upstairs to purchase some batteries, which we did. We got to the counter in the TV area, and no one waited on us. All the TVs were on, and there were people watching them.

I glanced at the screen and saw the front part of a blue truck that may have collided with something. It really startled me, and I wanted to leave. Then it got worse; there was a crash—the truck noise. I completely lost my composure and was very frightened. I burst into tears and asked Ernie if we could leave. (I'm not so sure about exposure therapy, at least for me.) The sight and sound of ambulances is also a huge negative trigger for me, which I must learn to overcome.

On May 25, I was in the kitchen and heard an airplane overhead. Later, as I was taking the ducks to the pond, the airplane flew right over me, very low and very noisily. I lay on the ground and cried. Why did it have to fly right over me? Then I crawled back to the house.

On May 26, the Disabled Adult Transportation System (DATS) picked me up for an appointment with physiotherapy. As soon as I saw the bus and driver, my body went into spasms, and I couldn't walk. I had done so well, and then I couldn't walk outside either. The bus had reminded me of an ambulance.

Later, when I was visiting my mom at St. Joseph's Hospital, I went to the chapel to pray. I usually went there with her. (She attended every Sunday.) This time I went alone, as I wanted to pray for a long time—so long it might be too much for her. I entered the chapel and immediately felt the presence of a higher power in a very secure, peaceful, and trusting way. I had so much to pray for. I thanked my heavenly Father for his love and nurturing during times of weakness. I prayed for my husband, our children, my mother, my siblings, their families, and I prayed for comfort for all the sick people in the hospital and everywhere.

I prayed that God would hear our prayers, no matter what our faith or wherever we were, that we could feel the presence of our one God within us all. I prayed for peace in the world, for the sharing of medical science, for world unity.

Sometimes I felt a magnetic force pulling me forward to the right or left, or backward. I had to concentrate very much and ask God to guide me. I thanked God for the health I did have and asked that I learn to accept my limitations and to be kind and helpful to others.

I left the chapel feeling very enlightened. I met a nun as I was leaving, and she said it was all right to go to the chapel. Then I visited with Mom. She hooked her rug, and I sorted the wool. Then I read from *Silent Unity* to her. And then the nurses come to help her get settled for the night and I leave.

May 27: It was Ernie's birthday. Sherry came from work at eight thirty after having worked a twelve-hour shift at the hospital. I didn't have to leave home, so it was a good feeling. I made Ernie a birthday cake and stuffed some twice-baked potatoes. We were having a family dinner, just the five of us: Ernie, Sherry, Carey, Cory, and me. Debi was invited but had to go to Grant MacEwan College, and Stu was expecting someone from Calgary.

It was a pleasant day, and my walking was good. Carey came home from work and barbecued, and Cory cut some grass and did some outdoor work. Sherry and Carey brought Ernie some patio chairs and end tables. Debi and Cory gave him an air compressor, and I a black shirt and tie. We enjoyed a nice meal, then Sherry left for work while Carey worked on his Jeep. It was so nice to see all the kids together—enjoying each other. It was a good day.

May 31: This was the day of Lisa's graduation party. Through hypnotherapy, I had been developing more confidence in my walking, so we attended the party. Ernie wheeled me to the door; I got out of the wheelchair and composed myself. I was in control because of hypnotherapy. We rang the doorbell, and as we did this, I heard a siren. Lisa's dad opened the door. I offered a handshake and then collapsed.

We didn't make a big issue of it, and although I required some assistance in steadying myself to and from the bathroom, we visited with everyone. The afternoon was splendid. But when we were leaving, I must have had some agoraphobia, as my legs were giving out on me. People helped me to my chair, but I would have liked to do it alone. However, progress was being made.

On June 1, I received a phone call from my lawyer advising that she was leaving the law firm in August and would like to take my file. We discussed it at length. I wasn't happy with the situation. She said I could go with her or stay with the firm I had retained. I asked if the case could be settled by August, and she said no. I consulted with Ernie, and we decided to stay with the law firm. (In hindsight, we should have gone with the original lawyer from the law firm; I think we would have had better results.)

Then, early in June, my bladder started aching badly. Sherry drove me to a walk-in clinic, where I was treated for a bladder infection. My body was riddled with pain. Then I had stomach and rib cage hurt. I was loaded with medication, and my tinnitus was unrelenting.

Lady wasn't doing well, though we took good care of her and groomed her often. She was very helpful to me when I couldn't walk, but that could no longer be expected of her. Despite this, she never gave up on helping me.

Cory took her to a veterinarian, where she was diagnosed with Cushing's syndrome and was prescribed medication. We couldn't afford the cost of her medications and the veterinarian bill but we did provide it for her and did all we could to help her survive but most devastating for us was to helplessly watch her suffer.

On June 6, I had an appointment with my hypnotherapist. We did a considerable amount of talking on this occasion. I told him how the grills of trucks and even vans bothered me. I also stated that one night that week I'd had a dream twice that I was dying. I had protected myself by covering my head. (Even at present my dreams and nightmares are horrible, and I usually dream of dead relatives, especially of my mother, my three deceased siblings, and Ernie.)

The hypnotherapist gave me a considerable amount of homework to do. I was to write three letters: to whoever I am angry or upset with; that person's reply; and the reply I would like to receive. I was also to draw pages and pages of car and truck grills. I did these assignments and still have copies of the letters I wrote, but those were only for therapeutic reasons.

The DATS driver was always upset about her boyfriend and was extremely verbose, but she wrote some nice poetry. On at least one occasion, as I recall, I was driven facing the back and observing all the traffic coming toward me. Those rides were more than I could bear. (It was not good exposure therapy for me.)

On one occasion in physiotherapy, I noted that there was a beautiful painting of a walkway in the woods. It looked comforting. I was stable that day; I worked at it. In one office, I observed paintings by Monet and Renoir, and I hoped I could paint someday.

When we got home, I wanted to walk in the woods but had to think of a place where traffic wouldn't upset me. I was in control. With my cane, I walked very slowly to the picnic area and fire pit. Lady came with me. It was blissful and beautiful.

I then said a long prayer for everyone in the universe. I felt the presence of God's love within me. I'm not a religious fanatic, but I do believe in the higher power. I prayed for God's guidance and thanked him for the nurture he provided.

When I was ready to leave, there was a squirrel on the table right beside me. Lady and I walked very, very slowly and went by the rock garden. I didn't know which direction to take, so we went over the bridge. It was all like a dream.

Later, Cory and Debi came over. Cory made me a salad and pizza. He still makes wonderful meals for me quite often and sends care packages of his gourmet food home with me for when I'm at the lake house. All three of my children do this. Their partners and my grandsons are gourmet cooks and prepare great meals, which I often enjoy; Ernie did as well. I am thankful for that.

Chapter 15

Middle of June 1992: In spite of all the goodness, I had depression and felt alone and lonely. Ernie was in Calgary, and I knew I had to get used to being alone and lonely. I had a lot of housework and laundry to do, and my day wasn't going well. It was eight-thirty, and I was finally on the last load of laundry. If I accidentally looked out and saw a truck, I would lurch and have increased tinnitus.

The next day, in midafternoon, I was alone and getting a panic attack. I tried to let it run its course, but I ended up calling my children. But I had a difficult time reaching them. No one knew of my problem at the time, and I didn't tell them. I was afraid I would upset them. I took my medication instead. Thanks, Zanax.

June 14: I worked in the rock garden and did quite well. Later I went to see the ducks with Ernie. Then I thought I would try walking to the journal box for the first time in a month. I couldn't. Ernie came and helped me but was very critical and annoyed with me, so I cried. All I seemed to do was cry.

The next day I had an appointment with my psychiatrist. He stated he had been to my hypnotherapist's seminar in Banff, was very impressed, and was sure the hypnotherapist would make me walk. I said I was also very pleased by the progress but was sensitive to anything that reminded me of the accident.

That night I went to bed listening to tape 2. Maybe I had come out of a trance too soon, as I had a headache and needed to take sleeping pills plus Tylenol. I had a very rough night— one of many. But I did feel I was making progress.

I had a multitude of appointments with my hypnotherapist, which were stressful but helpful. He wrote quite a comprehensive and accurate report to my lawyers indicating I had made significant progress but would require further follow-up. That follow-up never transpired.

For therapeutic reasons, as I mentioned previously, both my psychiatrist and my hypnotherapist advised me to write letters to the people involved in my accident. I can't understand why these were never sent in reality. I'll quote only one, written to my lawyers:

June 11, 1992

To: My Solicitors

This is in reference to the accident I sustained on April 27, 1989, which you are acting upon on my behalf.

I feel the time has come where I must emphasize some of the grievances and circumstances to give you and the insurance company involved a clearer picture of the hardships this major event has imposed on my family and myself.

Needless to say, this has caused me, and continues to cause me, considerable pain, fear, and anger, which I have been living with since that occurrence and I am trying to cope with and recover from. I am upset with the driver who struck me, but what has been done cannot be undone and I am certain the extra stress he may be experiencing cannot be very helpful to his state of health either. Hence, his insurance company should, without reservation, be actively involved and concerned with both his and my well being. Is this not why one carries automobile insurance?

For certain, the trauma I experienced through this injury has turned my family's and my life upside down. This devastating experience has led me from living a fulfilling and rewarding life one day, to nothing but unrelenting grief and all that goes with it, thereafter. Firstly, the fear, pain, tinnitus, problems with ambulating (to name a few), the various medical and physiotherapy appointments, the development of agoraphobia—trying to understand it and learning to live with it, and hoping that others understand, the numerous hospital admissions, etc., is not anything I would ever, ever, want to relive and

I certainly would not want to wish it upon anyone. The headaches, nightmares, sleepless nights, muscular pain and spasm, and the numerous medical problems, many of which still besiege me now. By way of this letter, I am back-lashing with considerable anger at anyone who does not realize that the past 3+ years of my life has been a life full of misery, to say the least.

The loss of gainful employment as a result of the accident, and the independence that goes with it, the fact that I can no longer apply the skills of my training and experience, having tried to do so, is not only a financial loss but also a loss of self-esteem.

Ernie's and my relationship is deteriorating as a result of the extra burden placed on Ernie because of my inability to be more self-sufficient and helpful. Ernie's state of health is questionable so this extra burden is difficult for him and has affected the whole family's life style.

The uncertainty of the status of my recovery is uncertain: i.e., will the tinnitus finally settle one day, or will it go on or worsen? Will I be able to walk as well as I used to, or will I continue to lurch and fall under certain circumstances? Will I have the strength I had before? Will I recover from my panic and fear without relying on medication to help me with this and with sleeping problems? I am concerned about the numerous medications I have been on and am still taking along with their side effects.

I miss being self-reliant and having to rely on others to drive me places. I hate to ask and thus I usually don't go. It is a lonely life. As much as I appreciate DATS transportation, the ride is rough and stressful for me, to the point that I dislike to go on it. It is not a permanent transportation system and does not provide an evening service where one could attend evening classes or support groups. However, I am usually too tired to go out in the evening anyway.

I am not accomplishing anything worthwhile as my energy is expended on appointments and minimal housework. I cannot look after our residence (inside or out) as I used to. If I have one or two reasonably productive days, they are followed by two or three days where I feel exhausted. I would love to work as I used to, or to paint and take classes, do volunteer work, or attend support groups but am unable to.

I am embarrassed by the way I walk and also cry when certain vehicles and other incidents remind me of the accident - being acutely sensitive to this. I do not think I or anyone else deserves to live this type of life.

The financial burden my lack of income has caused is another factor which has a tremendous impact on the way we live, as I was earning approximately $30,000 yearly, based on a four day work week.

Primarily, I am disappointed in the way the insurance company has procrastinated in assisting me voluntarily, or otherwise, in an obligation that is rightfully theirs, leaving me no choice but to place the matter with an attorney.

I wonder if this is the norm for the way insurance companies treat individuals who have been injured by their insured? Should this be exemplary, I would expect there must be a tremendously low morale between the insured and the insurance companies. Why the long delay in meeting at least some of their obligations, and doing so without reserve, but in a forthright, responsible and respectable manner. For instance, I have paid approximately $400 for physiotherapy, but was the insurance company at that time concerned? It would appear not.

In closing, I can only reiterate my disappointment in the procrastination by the insurance company which is frustrating, leading to stress, as we all know.

It is not a great letter, but it addresses some of the issues that were concerning me at that time.

June 26: I called my lawyers and asked for an advance. It didn't happen. Our taxes were due on June 30th, and we were in a desperate situation.

The next day, I was tidying bedrooms. When I was in Ernie's room, I heard a loud noise, looked out, and saw a huge airplane coming right at me. I quickly shut the patio door, lay on the bed, and was plagued with tinnitus. It was a long time before I could walk again. Ernie walked in and gave me confidence, and I tried to iron and listen to one of my hypnotherapist's tapes.

I was asked to record my dreams. They were mostly nightmares, but one morning I vividly recalled a pleasant dream. I was at a large gathering. My late brother, Bill, was there. I was hugging him and so happy to see him. He was young, dressed in a white shirt and tie, and looking for our mom. She was young and smiling.

Chapter 16

One morning I was determined to go to the ducks on the pond. I did, and I let them out of their enclosure. I was watching them when out of nowhere a deer was standing there. It started coming toward me—and I toward it. It became frightened and ran away. The ducks swam toward me, and Lady was with me too. It was so pleasant and calming. It was strange too because just the day before I had created the image of a buck and a doe in one of my paintings, and the deer looked just like the deer I had painted. It was almost like a dream. Carey has that painting now.

The next day I was going downstairs, and there was a rabbit right off the front deck on the shale. I watched it for a long time, and then it trotted off. Then there was a squirrel. Nature is so beautiful, with all the birds and animals. Nothing hurts you.

I find peace and solace in the woods. It's a great place to pray, and I can feel a certain closeness with our maker and express my feelings, my gratitude, and yet still my pain, which is hard to do. But I do try and am getting stronger. Though sometimes I feel weak and vulnerable, I'm not as afraid as I used to be.

June 25, the day after my birthday, I had a difficult time facing this morning. Vicky phoned and thought I was coming over to paint. I couldn't, but we had a lengthy telephone visit. Then I tidied up a bit and went to see the ducks. It was difficult getting there, but I made it and enjoyed being close to nature. Coming back I wasn't so lucky; I practically had to crawl back. The sirens, car grills, and noise all made it difficult. I went back and spent the rest of the day trying to do the vacuuming—always on my knees. Then Cory and Debi came and brought me a beautiful book, *Earth*. I love books, and I thought maybe I would paint something from it.

I feel the need to enclose this in my memoir. When Carey was aged two he had a traumatic health experience. It began on a Sunday at about 4:00 pm when he became acutely quite ill. Ernie and I cancelled our dinner invitation to be with Carey as his condition appeared to be worsening. We called the doctor who made a house call, examined Carey and advised us to take him to the hospital emergency without delay as he suspected meningitis.

On arrival at the Royal Alexandra Hospital Carey was admitted, examined, and placed in an oxygen tent with his arms supported to the sides of the bed. The nurses said they would check on Carey hourly. Through a slit in the oxygen tent I was able to hold Carey's hand and observe him. I noticed that his breathing had become extremely labored, he was pallid and his face was turning blue. *Carey had stopped breathing.* Ernie bent over Carey and I thought he was kissing Carey goodbye but he was administering mouth to mouth resuscitation.

Carey was rushed to the Intensive Care Unit (ICU.) while we sat in Carey's room through the night in total despair at possibly losing our child. Finally, at 6:00 am we were notified that Carey was revived and had survived. His difficulty was that he had acute tracheal obstruction with a glob of mucous lodged in his throat.

Thankfully to God, to his doctor, and the staff in ICU, Carey's life was saved. I have sincere empathy for anyone who loses a child; it must be so devastating. Carey is able to recall the incident and it has created a special bond with our dear Carey. This transpired many years ago.

On a special occasion, Ernie, Sherry, Stu, Debi, Cory, and Carey took me out for dinner at the Ginger House, Sherry's treat. The ride was bad, but it was a very nice dinner and great to be with my family. It had had been ages since I'd seen Stu. He and Sherry looked happy together, and that pleased me. Cory and Debi looked content with each other too, and Carey (happy Carey) said it was great to be single. I think he meant it. So nice to get out with everyone and that they all get along.

However, in spite of the comfort of family and nature, my problems with PTSD, panic, and agoraphobia continued. One day in October, I was getting ready for physiotherapy. I walked down the hallway and was fine. Then a car drove quickly by, my walking changed, and I started to have a full-blown panic attack. Also, some other vehicles driving by startled me. I closed the shades and went down to take my medication.

I was becoming very frightened. My arms and legs were cold and turning numb. I rushed and took a Xanax. Smart move. I knew I couldn't go to physiotherapy, because I was all stressed out.

I then had an experience just like the time I was admitted to the University Hospital. I stood at the kitchen window and prayed for the universe—for everyone. I was shaking and crying. I was afraid I wasn't going to make it. Sherry came down, and I hugged her.

It's difficult for others to understand my panic. Who can? Even I can't. Ernie had difficulty with it. When I panic, I think all sorts of bad things will happen to my family or to me. I was having more and more of those feelings, but usually I could prevent them from worsening by doing something positive—but it was so difficult.

Many, many times I said long prayers, thanking our heavenly Father for the beautiful universe and all that is within it. I felt a comfort and closeness with God, and I prayed that we could have unity with our one God, that humankind could work together and share knowledge. I prayed for forgiveness of sins, mine and others'. I prayed that we could help one another, rather than destroy. I thanked God for my life and prayed that I could accept whatever was willed for me. I prayed for my family, for all humankind, and, yes, for the birds and the trees and the seasons that come and go. And I prayed for strength so that I could help others.

I had numerous appointments and impositions on family and friends that haven't been recorded. Starting in the fall of 1992, I had to be accompanied to all my appointments. No one was compensated. That's the year I went to Red Deer College for an art course, but I didn't do well because of agoraphobia and panic. But I did create a huge oil painting of our acreage.

My lawyers advised that everything was going well, and they wondered who would be the best person to represent me, my psychiatrist or my psychologist (who did hypnotherapy). It didn't seem to matter, so I said, "I hope they would both treat me the same way."

On November 2, 1992, I was admitted to the Royal Alexandra Hospital and discharged on December 8. Discharge diagnosis: ataxia, gait disorder, monitor medication.

Chapter 17

With some reservations, I've decided to quote part of the interim report made by the hypnotherapist. It was dated March 23, 1993, and was sent to me by my lawyers. It was lengthy and accurate, but I quote only the last two paragraphs. (I had seen this psychologist in treatment for twenty-four sessions.)

This is an extremely complex case of dissociative paralysis with agoraphobia and panic attacks, all of which are directly resultant of her having been involved in this motor vehicle accident. Prior to this event she would appear to have been functioning quite normally and was working effectively as a medical dicta-transcriptionist. As you can see from the extensive work that has already been done to get her to the point where she is now able to leave my office and walk a distance of about 25 yards to the waiting room, put on her coat, walk outside, take an elevator downstairs, etc., as well as reportedly walk more freely within her home and about her home, although restricted in the latter case to a particular area away from vehicles, it will continue to take a great deal more work to hopefully get her to a state of greater independence. I am, however, of the opinion that it is highly unlikely that this soon to be 59 year old woman will ever return to the competitive work place. In addition to dealing with the dissociative disorder, the problem associated with anxiety, panic and pain also must be dealt with. This may take anywhere up to another year or two given the rate at which we are proceeding. I would accordingly estimate that it may take between $7,000 and $10,000 in fees to provide her with the necessary psychotherapy and hypnotherapy required over this next time frame. I believe that is a reasonable process to follow as short of working on developing a greater degree of independence, it would be necessary to provide an aide into her home so that she may feel safe when her husband leaves the home. We simply cannot take the risk of her crawling out into the yard and facing hypothermic conditions in the winter time if this pattern persists. It may still be necessary periodically to have access to someone coming into the home on a periodic basis so as to allow her husband to leave the home for short trips as he wishes to develop a realtor practice.

I am certainly prepared to continue working with her as I believe some progress has been made. I understand that you are entering in to settlement discussions at this time and will await your further direction. If this matter were to go to trial, I believe it would be helpful to conduct a further psychological assessment which I would certainly be prepared to do so as to provide you with a pre-trial report as I regard this one to be an interim report describing her therapeutic process.

I didn't see this psychologist in follow-up, as he had recommended.

In the medical reports requested by my lawyers and the defendant's lawyer, the diagnostics were accurate. But the impression of me as a person in some cases wasn't very constructive. I was apparently classified as whinny with a "poor me" attitude and as someone with a lifelong personality disorder. As stated in one report requested by the defendant's lawyer, I was hypochondriacally doctor shopping prior to the accident.

This saddened me because all those appointments were arranged for me by either mine or the defendant's lawyer. The appointments were stressful and difficult, but I complied, and prior to the accident I hadn't seen my family doctor in three years and didn't even know who it was.

In November 1993, I wrote the following letter to my lawyers:

Dear Sirs:

Needless to say, I am frustrated about the time frame already being five years, only now to be informed this will take another two years to be settled. In the five years that have elapsed and with the care I have received and in many instances have not received my life has become totally lacking in quality despite all my efforts to be as I was prior to the accident of April 27, 1989.

During the upcoming meeting with yourselves on November 26th, following are some of the areas I would like to be made more comfortable with:

I continue to try to overcome the two greatest factors which are fear of vehicles that I cannot overcome, and my panic brought on by the thought of something harmful happening to myself or other members of my family. The panic I feel is so overwhelming that I cannot be left alone, am disturbed and panic at the sight of vehicles, especially their grills. I cannot walk past them or go near them. After any trip that I take in a car I am totally unable to walk. Consequently I am living the humiliating experience of having to crawl on my hands and knees entering homes, in my own front yard and in my back yard when vehicles drive by. This has caused me an overwhelming loss of self-esteem; all along anticipating this would be temporary and I would recover. However one has to face reality and it has now been approximately five years since the accident with no improvement but rather some regression.

I know that I could have been in a position to recover and somehow feel that my life, in a file form, has been sitting on the back burner and I wonder why, when I personally know that many recommendations, both by the reports of the defending counsel and yourselves, could have enhanced my recovery markedly had the advice been heeded.

I attended every appointment that I could and was referred to, followed the advice given, and tried to be patient and at the beginning just still being thankful to be alive and thinking I would soon recover. Well, I haven't!

I tried to work and am not to be faulted for that. My regular family doctor was on leave and I took whatever advice was given to me. I took time off work, I tried to work, I took time off and in hindsight feel perhaps I shouldn't have gone back to work at all. But the damage was already done by my being struck by that 1/2 ton truck on April 27, 1989.

Nothing positive came from this letter.

I kept some diaries in 1993 and 1994, but I don't know what happened to them. I felt I didn't want to continue keeping diaries, because nothing improved. Most of my falling occurred where there was traffic, sirens, or airplanes. At home I would pick myself up with the help of Lady, who died because we couldn't afford proper veterinarian care for her. I was so saddened by her loss. (In hindsight I feel we did the best we could have done for her under the circumstances; she was so important to our family.)

I noted I had taken 336-plus containers of prescribed medications and some over-the-counter analgesics when I so much wanted to stop taking them. I only ended up with setbacks and pain. I was hoping someone would steer me off medications. It helped stabilize me to some extent but was very costly with side effects. I wondered if there was a medication I hadn't been on for my affliction. I didn't abuse them; I took only as prescribed. At times I felt I was rallying, but I hadn't recovered from PTSD, muscular pain, spasms, and depression.

There was no offer of assistance of any source, no help with house or yard work, transportation, or food. Our Visa bill escalated to more than $15,000, and the bank refused to carry us. Most of our payments covered only the interest, which was huge. We were losing our home because we couldn't afford to make the mortgage and other payments that were required. Despite repeated requests through our solicitors for funds to help us along, nothing was forthcoming, except for one advance of $10,000, which partially paid some outstanding bills.

As a result of all the above, I became alienated from and a burden to my husband. Two of our older children lived a considerable distance away from home, and only our youngest was with us in Sherwood Park for awhile. A thirty-five-year marriage had crumbled because I had changed. I wasn't bringing home a salary, and we needed both salaries to survive on the acreage. I was dependent on others to help me, where I had always been capable and independent.

I wasn't and never have been a malingerer. I did everything I possibly could to get well and support myself. It hurt to think I might end up in a home because of my health issues, which brought on a fear of living alone. It was neither my husband's nor the government's responsibility to provide for my care; neither was it hardworking taxpayers responsibility.

I worried whether I could go on living on my own—physically and financially. I knew my husband shouldn't be forced to selling our home. The painful breakdown of our relationship that was once so strong and secure was finalized on April 27, 1989.

Chapter 18

I hadn't had a vacation in six years, but in 1994, my sister, Stephanie, who had malignant breast cancer, very kindly offered to take me to Hawaii with my wheelchair. That vacation was a blessing full of everything good, including prayer. We went to the beach, I in the wheelchair.

One day I was walking along the railing by the ocean, and when the railing ended, I just continued walking. The sun, the beach, the fresh air, the ocean, and no traffic—it was miraculous!

I sent many postcards home announcing this and was sure I was on my way to recovery. I believe I even sent one to my solicitors. One of the lawyers stated later, as I recall, that I was "running on the beaches of Maui."

Well, I hadn't recovered!

Very shortly thereafter, on November 16, 1994, my husband and I were contacted by my lawyers with a presentation of a settlement in the amount of $110,000. We were given ten days to accept this offer, or it would be withdrawn. In our desperate financial situation and because of my mental and physical status, there was little choice but to accept it. This is the calculation they used to arrive at the net sum of $110.000:

> General damages for pain and suffering, loss of amenities, and loss of enjoyment of life: $73,000.

> Loss of earnings or earning capacity, past and future (including interest calculation with respect to past loss of income): $290,000.

> Allowance for care requirements, past and future: $35,000.

> Total: $398,000.

LESS: One-third reduction having regard to the issue of liability: $265,000. [I thought that was fair; the liability factor involved both the driver and me.]

LESS: 50 percent based on the issue of causation [that is, conversion hysteria and associated psychological components]: $132,500.

LESS: Advances under s.321 of the Insurance Act and Section B disability benefits: $25,600.

NET: Amount offered of $106,900 rounded to $110,000.

The lawyers should have been cognizant of my diagnoses as a result of this injury. They repeatedly received hospital, medical, and consultation reports identifying my diagnoses. This is how little they knew or cared about the afflictions of PTSD, agoraphobia, conversion reaction, depression, and all the diagnoses as outlined in the hospital, medical, and consultation reports they received and which they, in turn, forwarded to me. My injuries and disabilities as a result of this accident were physical, psychological, and financial, and then they reduce my claim by 50 percent because of this. Where was justice?

After their withdrawal of advances under s321 of the Insurance Act and Section B disability benefits, they issued a check for $89,066.59 on December 8, 1994.

Alberta Health and Wellness's subrogated claim was in excess of $107,000 if paid in full. After negotiations, which I wasn't involved with, the claim was reduced to $20,000, which Alberta Health and Wellness accepted as paid in full. Why? All of these expenses were a direct result of the accident. The lawyer's statement also said that interest incurred on my behalf was approximately $9,500, and that interest was waived. Again, why?

When retained, our lawyers stated they would be representing only us. But they also represented Alberta Health and Wellness, which I believe is a conflict of interest. If not, it should be. In accepting a reduced settlement by Alberta Health and Wellness, this reduced what would have been payable to me.

I found this out later in some documentation from my lawyers, as I was planning on writing a memoir because I was clear-minded.

On November 16, 1993, in their affidavit, which I paid little heed to at the time because of my mental instability, I found that the lawyers assessed my claim at $550,000 to $1,500,000.

Included in the amount was this: "aside from damages for pain and suffering are damages for cost of care, and loss of income (past and future)."

Also on November 16, 1993, their Amended Amended Statement of Claim stated,

> Leonora Diepenbeck (also known as Leona) Claims: General damages in the sum of $1,500,000.00 for inter alia, pain and suffering, loss of amenities and enjoyment of life, cost of future care and loss of future income, also:

> Special damages in the minimum sum of $152,289.38 and other damages as deemed at trial.

The trial was scheduled to go to court for fifteen consecutive days and was to commence on May 29, 1995. I advised my lawyers I was willing to go to court, but that never happened. The lawyers stated they would provide me with a discontinuation of action once filed. I never received it. It would be interesting to know what transpired in the assessment of those claims.

I grieved many losses and still do. I've pondered endlessly whether it would be appropriate to disclose the financial aspect at the time of this writing. This isn't so much a monetary issue but a disclosure of the variation in the differing assessments of my claim by my lawyers, so I believe it's relevant. For example, the Unjust Release stipulates, in part,

> It is understood and agreed that this settlement is the compromise of a doubtful and disputed claim and that neither the payment of the settlement monies nor the acceptance of this document by the parties released herein is to be construed as or deemed to be an admission of liability on the part of the parties released herein, by whom liability is expressly denied.

And the lawyers representing me condoned this!

Image related to PTSD

This is where I first started walking, unaided, along the railing in Hawaii

Image related to PTSD

These are just some of the medications I had taken

Chapter 19

It is my hope and plea that someone responsible, qualified, and caring—perhaps our own minister of justice, provincial and/or federal, would make an expected and much needed review of some of the frailties within the justice system and what appears to be the outdated and unfair Statute of Limitations, in which lies a grave injustice. A review of the negligence of some lawyers and insurance companies is also of utmost importance and appropriate. If the review of the Statute of Limitations is accomplished, those who have also appealed for justice, yet been neglected, would benefit from a well-substantiated review and outcome.

***

As I mentioned previously, many of my diaries disappeared, and all I recall is heartache. Ernie's and my marriage was deteriorating rapidly. I have a few brief annotations from 1995, which I'll refer to only with a great deal of hesitation. Ernie was very unhappy with me and wanted me out of his life, and he didn't hesitate to let me know it.

I hate to be critical of Ernie, as he certainly had his attributes, but he just couldn't cope with my inadequacies any longer. It was also difficult for me, as I was being put down frequently. In May 1995, I noted that Ernie had been very mean to me for the past week, calling me every awful name one can think of. I couldn't stand to be put down so badly, especially when we were in the car. It hurt so much, I had to become independent.

He kept asking what he was going to do with me and where I wanted to live, as he wanted his freedom. He said he would be nice enough to find me a place. When I crawled into bed to try to get settled, he said, "Stop it, or I will hit you." I dreaded sleep, because he hit me and pulled my hair, because—he said—I snored and awakened him. He said he was a light sleeper, yet it was all right for me to listen to his snoring for over thirty years. And because he was such a light sleeper, I don't think he got up once when the children were babies and cried all night. I was nursing and was literally worn out because they had colic.

I also worked throughout our married life until my accident of April 27, 1989. I was so lonely and hurt so deeply. I didn't know if I could ever please Ernie or at least be treated like a human being. I went to bed playing love songs with an aching heart.

I tried to attend group support meetings at the Charles Camsell Hospital, the Grey Nuns Hospital, and the Clinical Sciences Building when I could, but I was having difficulty walking. On several occasions, paramedics were called to help me. They would put me in a wheelchair, which I often resisted, explaining to them that this was a frequent occurrence and not to worry. Someone, usually a stranger, helped me, but I was getting worse. I worried about making a scene, and then it happened. Because my ability to walk had gradually regressed, I just couldn't make my legs to function well.

On one occasion, I saw Ernie in the yard with his hand on his chest. I thought he may be having a heart attack, so I went out. But by the time I got out there, he was nowhere in sight. I then heard a terrible noise coming from the road. I walked toward the road, looked up, and saw a huge truck in the yard across the street with a monstrous grill. I was terrified. I screamed and ran backward all the way to the house. Stevie called me while I was having the panic attack. She had difficulty understanding my fear.

At times, strangers drove me home when they saw me lurching and falling, because they didn't think I should drive. Every morning, I awakened with panic. At the end of May, I was attending a class, "Friends of Fear," in which a nurse demonstrated acupuncture. I left early and walked out of the area perfectly well.

When Debi and another girl caught up with me and remarked about how well I was doing, I lost my balance. A campus security driver drove up with his vehicle, which looked like an ambulance. I fell, and it required four people to get me up. It was very stressful. The security driver helped me to my car, and another vehicle drove up. I went down again. I hated making a scene! And this was one of so many similar instances. I was also constantly on a multitude of medications for my continuous health issues.

On August 18, 1997, I finally wrote a much-needed letter to the president of the insurance company that represented the defendant, outlining what had transpired since the accident. The response I received was very brief, terse, and negative. He was sympathetic to my situation but stated that I was represented by a leading law firm and should contact them, which I did.

In my contact with the law firm I had retained, the lawyer stated he couldn't help me but could refer me to someone by the name of Mike at the Alberta Mental Hospital.

I then met with the lawyer who was originally with the firm. She said she couldn't help me because it would be a conflict of interest. I failed to understand that statement. I recall falling flat on my back in her office. No one would help me.

This is how I was treated by both the law firm I had retained and the insurance company involved.

My sister, Stephanie, who was very brave and supportive, was suffering from malignant breast cancer. She was everything to me: my best friend, my soul mate, my confidant. She really cared, and vice versa. Because of my difficult mental and physical state of health, which unfortunately wasn't well understood by some, I was unable to visit her as often as I would have liked.

Stephanie passed away in my arms on May 24, 1998. The last word I heard her say was "Leona." I miss her dearly. It's my prayer that her beautiful spirit has moved on to greater dimensions, encircled and protected by God's everlasting love. I grieve the loss of my dear sister so very much.

Also, in 1998, Ernie's and my marriage reached an all-time low. I was spending most of my time alone, especially weekends. At that time, I learned through an anonymous telephone call that my husband wasn't always working in Calgary or at trade shows. He was spending his time with another woman. I was devastated; I felt neglected and unwanted. Ernie and I were legally separated but never divorced.

I summoned up strength and courage, and with my limitations and shortcomings (my walking had improved), I had no choice but to remove myself from that situation. Losing and leaving my marriage as well as our beautiful country estate was the most difficult and saddest thing I have ever had to do.

Part 2

Chapter 20

In Edmonton, I lived at two different addresses. First I was in a high-rise apartment on the top floor. I wanted to be as high up and as far away from everything as I could be. I had a view of the river valley and went on long walks when I could, enjoying nature, but I was very lonely and depressed. I could afford to live in that unit only for a few months. Then I moved to a lower unit that was very dismal and had mice under the kitchen sink and in the closet.

I became more depressed and was failing mentally. I was fearful, and on at least two occasions, in a panic, I slept in my car. I made it difficult for Cory, who subsequently helped me move to a senior's residence. I was again having difficulty with balance and with being unable to walk properly. I did some painting while at that residence but still missed our country home and the natural habitat surrounding it.

At that time, Ernie had sold our acreage home at a very depressed price. But with some income from that sale and from a stock, which I was fortunate to have held and which had gone up in price, I was able to purchase the condominium in 2000 in which I still reside. I've had many difficulties while living here, mentally, physically, and financially.

In 1999, I was admitted to the Grey Nuns Hospital, which I can vaguely recall. I have no hospital records from that admission.

In 2001, I was a patient at the University Hospital from July 16 to October 10. I don't have records of that admission either, but it was related to my previous diagnoses.

In 2003, I was under the care of another psychiatrist, who treated me well, both as an in-patient and an out-patient. This is a copy of his consultation medical report dated July 30, 2003:

Mrs. Diepenbeck is a 69 year old woman who is separated from her husband and who lives alone in a condominium in Edmonton. She was referred for further assessment and evaluation of current medical treatment. Most recent treating psychiatrist could not see her until the fall of this year.

Mrs. Diepenbeck presents with a longstanding history of anxiety, mood dysphoria and depressive symptomatology in context of apparent brain injury post MVA in 1989. She apparently had post traumatic panic syptomatology as a result of that accident. Similarly she has had major and significant psychosocial losses as a result. She lost her marriage and has been separated from her husband for a number of years. She lost her home on the acreage and currently lives in a condominium alone. She lost her job as a medical transcriptionist. Similarly she continues to grieve the loss of her sister who passed away five years ago who was a great support to her. Additionally, she apparently had a mastectomy for breast cancer a year ago.

Most recently she has continued to struggle with ongoing depression and anxiety. As mentioned, she continues to grieve many of her losses. She does admit that loneliness and demoralization has been a big problem of hers. She does feel significantly supported by her three children however, in addition, she has had to struggle with frequent falls secondary to ataxia. She did have significant problems with ongoing tinnitus for a number of years but this has improved greatly with the use of medication.

Most recent concerns have revolved around anxiety and fear regarding further tinnitus. There had been further concerns regarding current medication regime, tired and fatigued perhaps secondary to medication changes when she was on a high dose of Aventyl up to 200 mgs at bedtime and up to 60 mgs of Celexa daily. These have since been decreased and she does state that she does feel significantly improved. She does continue to have some anergia. She complains of loneliness yet she does have some social connections and supports. She has done numerous support groups in the past. She continues to be involved with a 60+ club and is quite involved with oil painting and personal instruction. Currently appetite is described as 'too good,' weight is reasonably stable and she would like to lose

15 lbs. She admits to craving sweets. Sleep is adequately preserved with current medication.

No previous psychiatrist history prior to MVA in 1989. Previously seen by a psychiatrist at RAH with previous diagnosis of Post Traumatic Stress Disorder and Agoraphobia. Previous admission to GNH in September, 1999. Also has two admissions to the UAH.

Past Medical History: MVA in 1989. Ongoing difficulties with mobility and apparent ataxia with frequent falls. Previous history of chronic tinnitus post MVA. Previous breast cancer with mastectomy, currently on chemotherapy (it was radiotherapy.)

Medications at Presentation: Aventyl 175 mgs qhs, Propranalol Triazide, Synthroid, Palaver, Detrol, Peridex, Arimidex, multi vitamins, Zyprexa 5 mgs qhs, Celexa 40 mgs daily, Clonazepan 1 mg bid.

Diagnostic impression: depressive Disorder NOS. Possibility of Organic Mood Disorder secondary to previous head injury and MVA/ Anxiety Disorder NOS, again possibly organically mediated with history of post traumatic anxiety. Dependent Personality Traits, History of MVA, History of breast cancer one year ago, Problems with primary support group and psychosocial environment and ongoing feelings of loneliness. Current GAF with moderate symptomatology approximately 55 to 60 at best in the past year 70.

Treatment Recommendations: I believe this woman has been treated very well medically over the last number of years. I suggested a serum Nortriptyline level at this time to further elucidate the nature of her Aventyl dose. I suggested continuing the current Celexa, Zyprexa and Clonazepan as before partly at her request. We suggested the possibility of START Psychiatry Day Program but she is not interested at this time. I suggested that a nurse should follow this lady. I could follow this woman and see as required in the future or I could see her periodically for the psychiatrist who had been seeing her before (but couldn't see her again until November.) Additionally, we thought that we could do an EKG as I could not find a copy since two years ago. I suggested that we could decrease the Rivotril somewhat and this might help her with ataxia however previous attempts at doing this had resulted in increasing anxiety. As mentioned for the most part I am happy with this dose and would leave it as is for now.

I am not certain who had given me a copy of this report.

In September 2002, the instructor from a painting class called me at home and asked me to discontinue attending classes because I was falling in class and I wasn't a good painter. This shattered my confidence in painting. Although I've created numerous paintings, mostly of nature and many of which I've given away, I have sold only one.

While living in Sherwood Park, I took painting classes and received some instruction and guidance briefly from Anne Derhak, Eileen Raucher-Sutton, Cecil Derkach, Lorraine Ure and a few other artists. In 1992, I enrolled in a session at Red Deer College, taking oil painting lessons from a renowned University of Alberta instructor. I also was a member of the Art Society of Strathcona County and had shown some of my work in their shows.

Although I enrolled in classes, due to my mobility and financial difficulties, I could not often attend classes or purchase supplies that were required. On the positive side, however, when I was engrossed in my art work I did not usually sustain flashbacks or spasms to my body. Painting was a form of therapy for me; with enthusiasm plus hard work I was able to create numerous oil and watercolor paintings.

When I relocated to Edmonton, I had a keen interest in art and became a member of the Art Gallery of Alberta. Because of my mobility problems—for the most part requiring a wheelchair—I had minimal showings there. I continued to paint but found it difficult to accomplish. I did my last painting in 2013. My hope is that sometime in the future I might exhibit some of my art work if I am able to do so.

I had no idea what I would do with my art. A lot of people thought it was quite good. But I didn't have the stamina to paint anymore or to try to sell some. As I wrote earlier, I painted a portrait of the accomplished singer, Bryan Adams, under some instruction. I was a great fan of his and spent many hours listening to his music, which helped me recover when I had a trigger/flashback from anything that reminded me of the accident.

When I was able to, I visited art galleries and frequented libraries to learn more about art. I was mesmerized by the accomplishments of some famous artists, but I was never satisfied with my own work.

**

I wasn't able to spend as much time as I would have liked with my mother, who was now very ill. She died on November 19, 2003. She was a pillar of strength to my siblings and me. I have nothing but good to say about her. I have some sad memories of her and my father, who passed away when he was only forty-eight, due to a coronary thrombosis. He was a farmer and a barber, and he was very creative, but because he was ill for so many years, my mother was required to work in the fields while we lived in the country and thereafter. But she managed to keep our family unit together in a very caring manner.

Going back to my health issues: does one ever recover—especially from PTSD? It appears not!

Art Work.

Art Work. Tree of Life, Version 1

Art Work. Tree of Life, Version 2

Art Work. Welcoming Spring

Art Work. You Shine so Bright

Art Work. The Acreage Pond

Art Work. Painting of 'Lady' in our backyard

Art Work. Canadian Rockies in Winter

Art Work. The Iris

Art Work.   Musical Genius. Bryan Adams

Art Work. The Iris

Art Work.   Musical Genius. Bryan Adams

Art Work. Escape

Art Work.   Winter Wonderland

Art Work.   Serenity

Art Work. The Beauty of Nature

Art Work.   Icy Splendour

Art Work.   Sand trap

Art Work. Cory's Golden Retriever Sammy

Art Work

Art Work. Our Acreage Home in Sherwood Park

Art Work.   My painting of the barn where I fell off the hay loft at the age of five

Art Work.

Art Work.   A Homestead

Art Work.   Part of the Homestead in Cadron, Alberta

Art Work.   How Steep the Climb

Art Work.   Blue Moon

Art Work.   A Beautiful Countryside

Art Work.

Art Work.

Art Work.

Art Work.

Art Work.

Art Work. Fearful

Art Work.

Art Work. Peaceful

Art Work.   Santorini

Art Work. A Beautiful Floral

Art Work. A Buck and a Doe

Art Work. A Cabin in British Columbia

Art Work. A Special Tree in British Columbia

Art Work. My painting of Lady in our backyard on the Acreage

Chapter 21

In April 2009, after a period of doing reasonably well, I went on a vacation in Arizona. While there, I suffered two full-blown, serious flashbacks triggered by the grills of two trucks. I just collapsed. My fellow vacationer, who drove a pickup truck that she referred to as a Jimmy, had difficulty understanding PTSD and its consequences. The people I was with treated me well, but I had difficulty recovering.

When we returned home, I took a turn for the worse and spent the summer at the Grey Nuns Hospital with a nervous breakdown. I was extremely traumatized. I thought my food was poisoned, so I wouldn't eat. I was afraid of medications. I developed incontinence. I may have been delusional, perhaps even psychotic. I was in constant fear. My family agreed to my having electroconvulsive treatment, and it was very difficult for them to observe what I was experiencing. Upon discharge, I was fine for a while but began regressing again.

That particular admission was an extremely difficult time for my family, me, and likely the hospital staff. Because of my altered state of mind, I would have weird thoughts followed by questionable actions. Primarily, when I saw my psychiatrist and my brother, Larry (Jim) discussing my prognosis, I thought they were plotting ways to get rid of me. I also had a severe hearing deficit and couldn't comprehend what was being said.

I wouldn't take my medications and refused to eat my food or drink my beverages—even water—because I thought it was all poisoned. My family brought me treats. My brother, bless him, even brought me fresh raspberries from his garden. I disposed of everything in the garbage bin—again thinking it was all poisoned.

I also entered other patients' rooms, disrupting them. On one occasion, I even climbed under another patient's bed, searching for someone famous who was supposedly going to save me and take me home. Recalling that painful time in my life, one of many, still saddens me.

The psychiatrist who was so instrumental in my temporary recovery was, unfortunately, not able to follow up on my care, as I was transferred to geriatric psychiatry upon discharge from that hospital.

In 2010, I was admitted to the Glenrose Rehabilitation Hospital from May 28 to July 6 because of flashbacks, depression, and insomnia. In the hospital, there were numerous triggers: ambulances, sirens, and truck grills There are so many incidents I could relate, but to what avail? The simple truth is that when I sustained the injury, I didn't know what had happened to me.

I know I'm reiterating now as I state that there was a man holding my hand and apologizing, very worried. I asked what had happened, and he replied, "You've been hit by a truck, and I am the person who hit you." Yet he denied it later. It was noted that he had a visual deficit, and I expressed my sympathy for that.

But where was justice for me? At the time, there was an ambulance, sirens, and a truck grill that I saw when I looked to see what had struck me. I believe there was an airplane flying overhead and the commotion of people in the parking lot. These are triggers that plague me even now. I hate to have to reiterate what causes my spasmodic flashbacks, which I don't know how to overcome.

I had another hospital admission in 2012, but I have no records of it. I believe I had a total of fourteen hospital admissions related to the injuries, physical and mental, that I sustained due to that accident. My latest admission was at the Villa Caritas in 2015.

I have regret. Because I was struggling physically, psychologically, and financially, I reached out for recompense, for justice, from 2010 to 2014. In December 2010, I contacted the then Minister of Justice who referred me to the Law Society of Alberta, which was unable to help me. They referred me to the Lawyers Insurance Association, which also was unable to help me. I then sent volumes of information to the Minister of Health, who was unable to help me. I wrote to the Chief Justice of Alberta and to the Premier of Alberta, who never acknowledged my correspondence, If I recall correctly. I even had one-sided communication with our then prime minister, who never acknowledged my issues.

Through advisement by some of these organizations, I contacted several lawyers, met them in their offices, and always broke down when I described what had happened to me and how I felt the lawyers and insurance company had failed me. They weren't able to help me, mainly because of the Statute of Limitations, which I should have been made aware of at the start of all my efforts to get assistance. Most felt that everything was done appropriately. One even condoned what I thought was a conflict of interest, which I referred to previously.

It wasn't so much financial recompense that I was pursuing. Lawyers and insurance company weren't appropriately seeing to my rehabilitation as well as not compensating myself or anyone else for all the losses. Because they weren't helping me in any way, I reached out to the aforementioned seeking justice, but I failed in all my efforts.

I regret that I didn't have the fortitude and stamina to spend those years more productively and in a more fulfilling manner, instead of pursuing justice. I can only console myself with the realization that I tried but just couldn't achieve what I tried to make right for others, especially my family, who also suffered losses in this sad account of events.

***

I experienced two serious falls in 2003 and 2004. The fall in 2003 reactivated the terrible tinnitus and muscle pain, and I had massage therapy treatments. I was on copious amounts of medication and suffered immensely. The one fall occurred while I walked outside a bank, in front of a truck. I had a flashback and fell on a steel pipe protruding from the sidewalk. I suffered a contusion too. I had multiple bruising as evidenced by an image taken of the gluteus area of my body.

When I go to that particular place now, I often have a spasmodic flashback that disables my walking. I received minimal compensation relative to those two falls, which only covered the cost of medication and therapy. I struggled from those falls for years and still do, with muscle pain.

The subsequent years in my condominium were very distressing as I continued to have flashbacks from truck grills, ambulances, sirens, the sign at West Edmonton Mall, and certain injury lawyers' advertisements (though those lawyers did me no harm). I was finding it extremely difficult to cope with my physical and mental impairments.

In order to be as functional as I could residing alone in my condo, I was driving my car, which was my safe place, as I was injured as a pedestrian. Because I constantly needed my wheelchair, that's how I got around. I struggled to put my wheelchair in the trunk of my car then drove to the mall to do my errands and to pick up my prescriptions and groceries.

I usually had flashbacks/triggers from vehicles at the mall. My body immediately went into spasms, and I couldn't walk. Sometimes Carey or my friend Jim would help me, but for the most part I was helped by strangers who were very helpful. I appreciated this, but I felt it was just not right for me to make these impositions on strangers and others.

Although I was in spasm I was able to drive my car with difficulty. When I would reach my condominium I had difficulty getting my wheelchair out of the trunk of my car and ambulating to my unit. I had to rely on others to help me, often strangers.

Chapter 22

From 2009 to 2010, the PTSD was so activated I was continually having flashbacks, falling, and crawling in my condo. This would last all day, and I'd crawl into bed at night, depressed, crying, exhausted, and in pain from the lurching and falls I'd had. Almost daily, I had flashbacks. I just couldn't go on living that way and ended up being in and out of hospitals.

One evening, as I was watching the late news, there was a program on near-death experiences. A man had been struck by a car and had terrible injuries. He had so many broken bones that it was amazing he was able to recover. I watched it, and when I tried to get up off the chesterfield, I was pulled backward several times. I spent the rest of the evening crawling, upset, and crying. I managed to get into bed by crawling around, but I had a terrible night with many tearful dreams. I now know for certain that my injury in 1989 was a near-death experience.

When I awoke, I faced the morning bravely. I took my medications and was having my usual healthy breakfast. As I always like to do, I read the *Edmonton Journal*. When I turned the page, there was an advertisement from another injury lawyer firm that I was not involved with. Even when they advertise on a television channel, I enjoy watching, but I try not to, because it almost always gives me a flashback of my injury and how my own lawyers didn't look after me.

I got off my chair and began lurching. It was already three in the afternoon, and I still hadn't had a shower or made my bed. I had to miss a barbecue in our Social Room because I couldn't walk. The spasm lasted all day. This is only one of so many similar incidents.

I had few friends in my condo, but one day three women were planning on taking me to Tim Horton's at the mall for coffee. I felt good about going. I phoned my friend Agathe, and she said that with three people accompanying me, I should have confidence that I would be okay. I agreed.

As I went downstairs, I was fine until I glanced out the door in the entrance and saw the grill of a truck. My body stiffened, and I thought I was going to fall, so I called out, "Grab me!" I was having a panic attack. One of the women went up to my unit and brought down my wheelchair, which I needed. They wheeled me into the mall, and we had coffee.

They were very helpful and kind, but I hated to have this happen and was afraid they might not ask me again. It was the only time since the year 2000 that I had lived in this complex that anyone had offered to walk to the mall with me. I was tired but thankful.

My unit is comfortable, but lonely. I think that's because some residents don't bother much with me because they undoubtedly visualize what a freak I am every time I come home with a spasm from a trigger/flashback I just experienced. Also, my hearing issues continuously fluctuate. One day I can hear very well, then for days and weeks on end, I can't hear at all, which makes communication extremely difficult or even impossible. But many of our tenants have been helpful.

However, a member of the board told me that I should seek a different residence to live in. I wonder where, and I wonder if I can afford what would be appropriate and right for me.

Chapter 23

I penned the following in October 2011.

I am tired of talking about my problems with flashbacks and spasms, which make it very difficult for me to walk and then I suffer muscle, back, hip, and leg pain. These triggers/flashbacks are recurring almost daily and I am quite run down physically and emotionally. Some medications have made me feel sad and more depressed, and I haven't been sleeping well

My doctor is trying to help me with medication, but I have been on so many medications for such a long period of time that I would hope for some other modality of treatment, but cannot afford the cost of expensive psychologists. I feel I have exhausted my children and I have few friends. I have a good friend, Jim, who understands my problem and I value his friendship. I told my doctor in visitation that I need more help with counseling and other modalities of treatment which I cannot afford.

The following I did not tell my doctor on this date and is quite repetitive of what I have previously stated. But I ask: "Where is justice?" We pay voluminous amounts of money to insurance companies for protection of those who have been injured but almost nothing came my way. At the time I was working, I was living on a beautiful estate which my then husband and I built and worked very diligently at. As a result of that injury, I lost my job, I lost the marriage because I was a mess, and subsequently my husband and I lost our home. The children suffered the losses too; it was difficult for them to watch me flounder around, in and out of wheelchairs, falling, crawling around when I would have a flashback and could not walk. I developed a severe case of tinnitus, I couldn't sleep, I had pain and spasms all over my body, I couldn't keep up with the house or yard work, I couldn't get to appointments that were set up for me as I had no way of getting there. I had no money for groceries. I was on huge amounts of medications, many of which had negative side effects, I was in and out of hospitals. I developed agoraphobia, post traumatic stress disorder, severe panic attacks and couldn't be left alone at home and would call my husband at work because I was so afraid. I had the comfort of our dog, *Lady*, and yet when she became ill I couldn't afford proper veterinarian care for her.

My husband had his hardships with me, but I don't think he ever really understood that I did everything I could to recover but just didn't have the support I should have had. I was asked to keep diaries by my lawyers which are astounding, and I don't know how I survived, but unfortunately no heed was paid to them. I was willing to go before a jury but this never happened and I don't know why. I have been on such profound amounts of medications that it is only when I am more clear minded that I realize now more than ever what a great injustice this has been.

Chapter 24

The following is from my journal.

March 7, 2013

I became aware yesterday that Ernie's malignant melanoma has metastasized to his brain, liver and lungs. [Ernie and I had become friends in recent years.] This is extremely upsetting. He was over for dinner tonight. He brought some marinated ribs while I made stuffed peppers. It was a nice, quiet time. He is extremely tired. Sherry will be taking him to the Cancer Clinic tomorrow to ready him for the radiotherapy he will have. His oncologist told him that if radiotherapy and chemotherapy are not successful he will have only four to six months to live and that he should get his affairs in order.

Ernie looked very ill after his radiotherapy of which he had several treatments to his head for the brain metastasis. He found it exceedingly difficult to walk. Carey dropped his dad off and then me. Carey also had come in to look at my computer as I was having problems with it. I mentioned to Carey that we need to consider the possibility of moving Ernie, his dad, to a place where he could have more care and meals provided for him. Sherry has been looking after food, appointments, library visits, etc. and I feel it is taking its toll on her. Ernie wants to stay where he is for now.

Yesterday Sherry picked me up and we went to Ernie's place. Cory and Kelly were there setting up Ernie's cell phone. Walker and Carson, our grandsons, were also there watching part of a movie. Sherry had brought a lot of supplies for Ernie. They were all very helpful to Ernie; they are good kids. I am trying very hard not to be depressed.

Talked with Ernie yesterday. He had an appointment at the Cross Cancer Clinic. He had a difficult time talking on the phone and told me that he had been given a three month survival as his cancer had metastasized considerably to his brain. I asked if he would like anyone to be with him. He says he just wants to be alone for now. Today he is having a difficult time but still wishes to be alone. I feel terrible for him and for all of us.

Today I went out for breakfast with Trudy from our condo. She is a very gracious lady. Her husband succumbed to dementia a few months ago.

May 8, 2013

Ernie is now at Norwood Hospice Care, which is palliative care. I spent a good part of yesterday with him. He is very quiet but appears to be comfortable. Yesterday he was visited by Sherry, Stuart, Walker, Carson, Carey, Tina, Cory, Kelly, and myself. It was a nice friendly visit for all. The kids are doing their utmost to be helpful. I'm still troubled with a cold/flu and am tired. I have had a few more incidents with flashbacks, but recover always.

May 11, 2013

Just returned from visiting Ernie at Norwood Hospice. Sherry and I spent most of the afternoon there. Stu, Walker and Carson came later. Walker had a great visit with Ernie, as they held hands—it was very touching. Ernie is trying to communicate with me but I don't quite get it. He wants to touch my breasts. I told Sherry I don't understand and Sherry thinks that perhaps he wants to acknowledge my breast cancer, which I had in 2002—which I have decided to acknowledge subsequently. Ernie appears quite agitated and has no movement in his left arm and leg. Sherry fed him supper—she is so excellent with him and I am so proud of her as I am of all three of our children, their partners, and our grandsons. Yesterday Ernie told me that he loved me. I have a lot of feelings for him too. Tomorrow our family will all be visiting.

In the year, 2002, I underwent surgery for carcinoma of the breast, followed by an augmentation procedure two years later. As I was being anesthetized for the second procedure, the anesthetist spoke the words "Good bye." I then spent five days recovering; had also been administered morphine. My body odor and food all had the same senses, horrible. I was delusional and required 24-hour nursing care. I was struggling and I would feel my body being compressed in a shaft, then it would rise to a room full of pink-feathered beautiful angels, then I would be struggling—compressed in the shaft again. I would be tied to a jerry chair, trying to escape. (Not certain why I am revealing this but perhaps because I am so painfully honest in my disclosures, just thought I would mention it.) Recovery was extremely difficult.

June 2, 2013

It has been almost impossible to write in my diary. Ernie had a very difficult time and so did we, his family. Someone from the family tried to be with him most of the time. He deteriorated quite rapidly and there was nothing we could do besides being with him, holding his hand, comforting him with kind words and prayers.

May 19, 2013

Most of us were with Ernie during the day. Sherry had left for home and at about 11:00 p.m. she had the feeling she should go back and be with him. She was with him when he passed away at 4:30 a.m.

It has been very difficult to function, let alone write. Ernie did not want a formal Service so our immediate family had a gathering in his Memory on May 25th at Stu's and Sherry's acreage which is what Ernie had wanted. It was very well put together with memoirs, photographs, and a special meal. Walker and Carson were very special to Ernie and vice versa which was very touching. Carson even wore a suit to the occasion.

Sad, but we will have many wonderful memories. Ernie was very intelligent and helpful in many ways; I will miss him terribly, and do already. I am also struggling with depression and grieving. My PTSD has lessened and I am happy about that. Maybe I am cured, I hope. Our children are devastated and their loved ones are very supportive of them. I am happy about that. Ernie is in God's keeping but he lives forever in my heart even though for so many years we were apart.

On October 28, 2014, I penned the following:

I need to be honest in stating that trucks, their grills, ambulances, and their sirens are not the only source of my PTSD. The sign "West Edmonton Mall" even on buses is still a problem for me as West Edmonton Mall is where the accident occurred. I do poorly on parking lots. Also the insurance company advertisements and signs will also cause triggers and spasms to my tormented mind and body.

I realize this all sounds bizarre but it speaks of truths and the problems I cannot overcome regardless of how hard I try. I feel I am driving away people I care about but I honestly cannot help what is happening to me. I have good days but they are unfortunately overshadowed by the dilemma I am encumbered with in my life as expressed above.

Chapter 25

In 2015, I began to regress and became quite delusional. I don't have a clear memory of what transpired, but I was apparently admitted to the Glenrose Rehabilitation Hospital in my delusional state. I vaguely recall that it was a very difficult time for me, my family, and likely the staff.

I couldn't be helped there, so I was transferred to the Villa Caritas Hospital, where I was from April 29 to October 7, 2015. When I was admitted there, I was apparently diagnosed as being psychotic, delusional, and depressed. On my initial arrival, I wouldn't eat or take my medications. I don't have much memory of my initial stay, probably because I received electroconvulsive therapy. My memory failed me so that I had no idea where I had formerly resided or what my residence looked like. I couldn't recall the doctors who had treated me, and I knew nothing about computers or cell phones. I had to relearn everything, and I'm still relearning.

In my delusional state, I had apparently told my doctor I was married to the singer Bryan Adams. I know; it's in the hospital records. This is embarrassing, but I hope I've always made it clear that I was captivated by his heart-rendering songs, especially the love songs, and that I'm a forever fan. This is an indication of how a mind is capable of conceiving a fallacy to be true in a psychotic and/or delusional state. Because of my traumatized mind and body, I wonder if in addition to my accident, all the meds I've been on over the years have contributed to my delirium. (But I must add that I believe the meds I'm on now are helping me.)

I was under the care of a very caring psychiatrist who, in about the middle of my stay at the Villa Caritas, acknowledged my PTSD as well, because I was having flashbacks, falling, and not walking properly. When I went on a walk on the hospital grounds and heard a siren, I fell to the ground, requiring my wheelchair. When I picked up a newspaper with what was for me a negative advertisement, I had a flashback and required my wheelchair. This continued. I required the wheelchair only when I had a flashback, but I had many. I was encouraged to use a walker, but when I had a flashback, I couldn't walk. It's difficult for some to understand this, though I try to explain how my body functions in strange ways when I have a flashback.

In August 2015, I started coming around. My family visited and took me out on weekend passes, which was difficult for them, because I usually had flashbacks after traveling.

I was then referred to a PhD psychologist at the hospital regarding the PTSD. She had me write and read about my problem. It was decided, at my request, that I write to the Minister of Justice and an MLA. The psychologist very kindly gave me the names and addresses, but I didn't follow through, unfortunately.

While at the hospital, I sustained a ruptured eardrum in my right ear. (I am deaf on my left ear.) I developed a severe infection accompanied by earaches. Even with the support of a microphone, which I had at the hospital, I had difficulty hearing. My daughter later bought me my own hearing device (not a hearing aid, as I couldn't wear one while my ear was infected). I found the patients and staff to be caring and kind, but because of my ear infection, communication was difficult.

I was discharged on October 7, 2015, to my condominium. I was given a Discharge Summary but am unable to locate it at this time.

After my discharge from the hospital in October 2015, while at an appointment with my family doctor, I found a brochure entitled "Alberta Ombudsman: Your Voice of Fairness." I read it and thought it would be appropriate to write the ombudsman about my problems relating to the unfairness following my accident of 1989. On October 17, 2015, I sent a lengthy letter. Clearly, as is evident; I wasn't giving up in seeking justice.

I received a reply dated November 5, 2015, stating:

> The Ombudsman has no authority to investigate complaints about insurance companies or lawyers. You may wish to bring your concerns regarding the law firm to the attention of the Law Society of Alberta; You may wish to bring your insurance concerns to the attention of Ombudsman for Life and Health Insurance.

There was no reference made to the settlement by Alberta Health and Wellness regarding their acceptance of $20,000 on a $108,000 claim, which I felt would have been under the ombudsman's jurisdiction. Their acceptance of this amount reduced what was payable to me. There was also a conflict of interest, as I had previously stated, as the lawyers were also retained by Alberta Health and Wellness.

Because I had already been repeatedly rejected by the Law Society of Alberta, I couldn't make any further attempts at seeking justice. So I decided to write this memoir in February 2016, starting with the accident on April 27, 1989.

Chapter 26

It has become apparent to me that twenty-eight years ago there was limited knowledge or concern among professionals about PTSD and some of the bizarre symptoms associated with it. For example, x-rays and orthopedic examinations don't aid in the diagnosis of PTSD. Unfortunately, there was—and to some extent there still is—stigma associated with mental health issues, and many sufferers are reluctant to admit to a mental health diagnosis. I've learned this through some of my own experiences.

It's my hope that anyone who is traumatized by what to them is a life-threatening experience will be guided to seek immediate professional help from those who are highly qualified in diagnosing and treating individuals with this affliction. There are psychologists who specialize in treating PTSD, but their care is costly, and that's part of the problem.

Through a referral, I had three appointments with a PhD psychologist. These appointments were extremely stressful, and I would break down when reliving the accident, verbally, with the psychologist.

This psychologist also treats those in military who have been afflicted with PTSD. The treatment focuses on prolonged exposure therapy (PE), which means facing your triggers. It also involves in vivo therapy. I have coverage for minimal treatments, and transportation is still a huge problem for me. But, I've made some progress in that I'm now able to push my wheelchair across a busy street to the nearby mall, walk across a parking lot behind my wheelchair for protection psychologically, with a multitude of vehicles parked there, pick up my prescriptions and groceries, and do other errands I haven't been able to do this in years. So some progress has been made, and I am optimistic.

I'm happy to have accomplished the above, but unfortunately I still have many triggers/flashbacks where I end up walking backward or sideways, crawling, with an aching body and depression. The positive part is that I'm able to recover much more readily from the flashbacks, whereas before I would remain in spasms till I went to bed at night.

I try not to refer to specific individuals I have been involved with since my injury, which is difficult to accomplish because many have been extremely helpful, and some still are. I'm fortunate to have loving children, their partners, and my two precious grandsons. They've been helpful in many trying ways, in the midst of some of their own difficulties, instead of my helping them.

I hope that readers realize that others struggle with PTSD and some of the bizarre symptoms associated with it. I repeat, in all I've learned about PTSD, I have not become aware of anyone having the symptoms of lurching, falling, walking backward or sideways, or having to crawl after having a trigger/flashback. It remains difficult for me and others to understand PTSD and all that it entails.

I must acknowledge a dear friend, Jim, who has been supportive of me for over ten years. He is intelligent, hardworking, and understanding of my problem with PTSD. He has helped me tremendously in the past when I encountered a flashback and couldn't walk. He says it's no big deal for him, but I dislike being an encumbrance, as I so often am. He has stated that these occurrences don't diminish me in his perception of me. I'm grateful for that, and I feel I should be acknowledging his assistance more, perhaps in a monetary way. Unfortunately, Jim now has health issues of his own.

I also give accolades to the help I've been receiving through Health Care and Pharmacy, which has efficient staff that are very helpful to me. I attend a very well-run senior's program and I have also attended a START program recently. I'm thankful to my doctors for their understanding, appropriate referrals most of the time, and prescribing and monitoring my medications.

I'm working on PE therapy, and my writing has been commended by my psychologist. I'm reading all the literature I find regarding PTSD, and I can fully relate to it. It isn't always effective, but I believe I'm making some positive strides.

I'm deeply saddened by the passing of my dear sister Kaye (Katrina) on March 3 of this year, 2016. She would have been eighty-eight on May 20th. I'm comforted by the feeling and prayers that she is in God's keeping, in heaven. What a wonderful humanitarian she was, and how she will be dearly missed! She was predeceased by her husband, Michael, our parents, and siblings, Stevie (Stephanie), Bill (William), and Ernie. My heart is with you, Katrina. You are dearly loved and always remembered for the kind and loving person you have always been.

I'm spiritually motivated and feel the need to express myself. I have compassion for the sad, the sick, the lonely, and the underdogs, who are less fortunate through no fault of their, own and due to unavoidable and unforeseen circumstances. I also have great empathy for those who have been unjustly mistreated and neglected.

I would so much like to say I've recovered, but my PTSD continues. Even though I now practice PE therapy, it might be a little late for me, as it doesn't always work. I don't know if one ever recovers from PTSD. Flashbacks from my accident continue to cause me to lurch and fall; I have difficulty walking, still having to crawl to get to my destination very often. I just can't seem to overcome this, and I'm troubled by depression and a feeling of loneliness.

I now have a wheelchair, a walker, a transport chair (used to get me to appointments because the wheelchair is too heavy for transporters to lift.) I appreciate the rides I do receive. I'm not able to leave my residence unaccompanied, which leads to isolation. But, on the positive side, I'm now able to wheel my wheelchair in front of me (for protection from facing traffic), cross a busy street and parking lot, and enter and walk into the nearby mall to do my errands. I hadn't been able to accomplish that in quite a while. I believe therapy and appropriate medication contribute to my accomplishing this. This, I believe, is repetitive due to some memory loss which I must admit to.

I'm still faced with imbalance and an aching body, especially with pain in my legs and hips. And I fall a lot. Because of this and the depression, I'm unable to accomplish much of what I would like to do. I'm now more insightful, and I worry about another relapse. I've had a total of fourteen hospital admissions related to the accident. *Where will I end up?* I wonder. I am also concerned about what I can or can't afford.

Along with PTSD, depression is difficult to understand unless a person is or has been afflicted with it. In addition to the flashbacks/triggers, depression can present itself as a profound feeling of aloneness and sadness, as it is for me. It's so difficult to achieve anything constructive.

Here are a few specific examples of how flashbacks and triggers have affected my body and mind recently.

1. I am outside. I see the grill of a vehicle, my body goes into spasms, and I walk backward to my transport vehicle. To enter a home, I can only crawl up the stairs and into the home to reach a chair. I sit there for hours, and I'm unable to hear anything or anyone all day due to a hearing impairment.

2. I'm attending a very well-run START Program at a hospital. I see a patient in a wheelchair; I collapse. I'm taken to a dance. Hadn't been to one in years. I love dancing; there was a live band, and I was able to have a few dances, without lurching or falling. When leaving, I see a wheelchair in the lobby of the hotel. I collapse and consequently I don't go dancing again.

3. My daughter takes me to an appointment. I pick up a magazine, as I love to read. I see what to me is a negative advertisement, and I fall down. She needs to bring my transport chair from her vehicle to ambulate me.

4. I watch a movie; see an ambulance on the screen, and hear a siren. I collapse and can't walk. I watch a parade on television; hear a siren and see an ambulance, also an insurance company advertisement. I can't walk and resort to my transport chair.

5. Very recently at the senior's program, which I enjoy, a staff member and a participant in the program offered to go for a walk with me pushing my transport chair on the beautiful grounds outside. Everything goes well until I see a truck approaching the intersection. My body goes into spasm and I cannot walk. I am walking again after seeing a pleasant sight—a puppy. This happened on two occasions similarly. On the second occasion I also have a trigger, see a pet dog that reminds me of *Lady—Our beautiful Samoyed. I am in my glory and walking again,* until I encounter the grills of a truck and the kind ladies are pushing me in my transport chair again. I hate being a burden and appreciate their help as I am unable to do this from my residence as I reside near a very busy street with no grounds to walk on and I can't do this on my own.

When my mind perceives a danger my body goes into spasm, causing me to fall or disable my walking. I want to emphasize how the component of PTSD affects me psychologically and physically, *Still!*

These incidents are not only painful and stressful but also humiliating for me and a burden for those who assist me. When my body is not in spasms, I can walk normally; that's why I'm not always in a wheelchair.

People say things like "Come on, walk; you can do it" or "You can walk; you just don't want to." That just doesn't work for me. My mind needs to be distracted by something positive, such as the enchantment of music or beautiful works of art, reading good literature, or being in the country, close to nature, seeing pet animals and birds, along with having the comfort of my loved ones.

I feel replenished when my family and loved ones visit—namely, Sherry, Stuart, Walker, and Carson, Carey and Tina, Cory and Kelly, and Jim—and take me to their residences. Many things distract me from my loneliness: kindness and comradeship; being outdoors, enjoying nature—especially being at the lake and on boat rides; my children's pets; the hot tub and sauna, which are so therapeutic; the special bedroom that I've been given by Cory and Kelly at their lake house; the outings with Sherry and family; the assistance with electronic devices by Carey; some photographic assistance by Julie (she also struggles with PTSD.)

I'm so thankful, and I try to be helpful when I can. I also appreciate being taken to a sports center occasionally by my good friend Jim, who also took me dancing.

As I have zealously sought restoration and healing for my afflictions over the years, I'm guardedly optimistic about what the future holds. This is enhanced by the reality that I believe it's time for me to acknowledge that the restoration of my mental and bodily health is difficult at this late stage, and there likely is no permanent cure for the encumbrance of PTSD.

With that said, I believe if PTSD is precisely labeled and treated at its earliest onset, with the advancement in medical science and research, it's prudent to be optimistic about rehabilitation of many who have been encumbered with this unnerving affliction.

I pray for God's blessings and world peace for all humankind
and everything within this universe; that we may all
learn to live in harmony with one another.

I will now endeavor to practice the discipline of
gratitude for all the positives in my life.

Epilogue

It's my hope that the readers of my memoir, especially those who might be afflicted with PTSD, have found it interesting and informative. Due to my aging mind and body, I don't expect to do any further writing. Thus, I provide below a brief but candid personal history and some noteworthy events in my life that might appeal to close family and friends.

I was born to the greatest parents ever, Metro and Maria Yakimchuk (also known as Yakemchuk.) My arrival was on a beautiful rainy day in June in Kahwin, near Andrew, Alberta, Canada. I identify myself as one of four siblings: Katherine, William, Stephanie, and Larry. When I was four, my family moved to Cadron. I attended primary school in Cadron and high school in Andrew.

In writing, I do not use descriptive modifiers that would enhance what I'm trying to express, such as used by more accomplished writers and that would likely make for a more desirable read. What I write is simplistic, but it is reality.

Following are a few incidents I relate to along with a little family history.

When I was delivered by a midwife in the country, my father was working away from home, splitting and hauling wood for our fireplace and stove. My siblings were so pleased at my arrival—I think—they wanted to do something special for our mom.

It was raining, and all the baby chicks had gotten out of their enclosure and were running about the yard. My siblings gathered the chicks, placed them in a bucket, and proudly presented them to our mom. But the chicks had all been smothered! Thrilled she wasn't, but they had tried so desperately to please her.

As a lover of nature, I would often go off into the woods, searching for wild strawberries, mushrooms, and wildflowers. I would be so entranced by being close to nature that I would be gone for hours on end. My mom followed my footprints to try to locate me. I still enjoy walking in the countryside and nature's wonders. It is so peaceful yet exhilarating.

At the age of four, I was attending an aunt's wedding reception at our home in the country. As I was standing in the driveway, a car driven by an inebriated and careless driver came barreling into the yard. A bridesmaid standing nearby saw this, and just as I was about to be struck down, grabbed my arm and saved me from what could have been a disastrous incident.

When I was five, my older brother, a cousin, and I were taking turns jumping off the hay loft in our barn onto a rack filled with hay. When my turn came, with a little help and encouragement, I jumped. But I missed the rack and fell to the ground. The ground was covered with rocks and pebbles. I sustained a ruptured eardrum that required three and a half months of hospitalization. I endured considerable pain and infections, but with the discovery of penicillin, I was treated and survived.

At the hospital, the doctors and nurses were very kind to me. The nurses gave me butterscotch candy, but I usually missed my desserts of ice cream because my doctor would call me in for an examination at noon. This I well remember. When it was time for my discharge from the hospital, my mother had no way of transporting me other than carrying me on her back to my maternal grandmother's home. My mother paid my hospital bills with produce from our garden.

This injury caused severe hearing loss, which affected my education, my social life, and later my employment, as I was always ashamed to admit to my hearing loss. Because of ongoing infections, in later years a complete radical mastoidectomy was performed, which left me deaf in my left ear. At present, I also have a perforated eardrum in my right ear with infections. A hearing aid doesn't serve me too well.

The foregoing is recent but related to my auditory problem. It has been almost impossible to get a referral to an otolaryngologist, in spite of my proclaimed grievances to various doctors over the years. I've struggled with discomfort, infections, and pain, often in both ears. In one appointment, I was apprised of an annotation in my file: "Leona is now in a home and will require no further appointments." Is this what we do with our geriatric patients and/or patients with mental health issues? I would hope not.

Finally, on May 1, 2017, through ongoing persistence, I acquired an appointment with an otolaryngologist. Upon careful examination, he discovered and removed a—*hearing aid*—embedded in my left ear. It had been there since April 24, 2011. I recalled the day it got lodged very well. I had been traumatized by a PTSD flashback as I was being taken in a wheelchair to a school to vote in our federal elections. All I knew was that I had lost my hearing aid. So for six years it had been lodged deep in my ear, yet all the professionals who had examined my ears missed it. I'm so thankful to this otolaryngologist and staff for their skill and caring.

Our family had and has a strong work ethic and utmost respect for parents and elders, but we lived in poverty and couldn't afford to pay our taxes. I remember my mother telling us that when the tax man arrived, informing her that he could place her in jail for unpaid taxes, she responded, "If you do, please take my children as well. At least they will have something to eat."

My father was very ill and was hospitalized at the time—one of many hospitalizations. My older sister, who was very intelligent, was unfortunately taken out of school at an early grade in order to help the family. My older brother suffered from rheumatic fever and was unwell a lot of the time. He later went to the city to attend university.

My mother was almost the sole provider. She labored in the fields and looked after my father's ailing parents and us children.

My father had a unique creative talent and built my brother's first violin. When he was well, he worked in a blacksmith shop, building buggies, sleighs, and cabooses, which were pulled by horses. We would ride in cabooses in the wintertime. A fire burned in a miniature stove that my father had fashioned for the cabooses. I have fond memories of that. My father was also the neighborhood barber.

Both of our parents were very hardworking and kind and lived solely for their children, which established a strong family bond. That has been so important to me, and it still is. They taught us how important work was in order to survive; we certainly did our chores. There were no handouts.

One freezing morning when walking to school, which was almost a two-mile hike, my hands were freezing and going numb from the cold. I entered a neighbor's home, and she placed frozen cabbage leaves on my hands to get the circulation flowing. At that time, the winters were extremely frigid.

I also recall an occasion when I had invited a school friend to our home for lunch. We walked through the fields, which took almost an hour. When we returned to school, we were so happy to hear the school bell ringing, thinking the lunch break was over—only to realize it was the end of the school day. I received a strap (a whipping) the next day—the only one ever! At that time, using a strap was acceptable punishment.

I enjoyed school, although often I had difficulty hearing my classmates and teachers. My teachers were great. I often invited them to our home for dinner.

I enjoyed the friendship of many schoolmates. My siblings and I were very close and had ongoing and rewarding friendships with each other. I also had a hobby of playing the mandolin.

At the age of sixteen, I relocated to the city, furthered my education, enjoyed a social life, and acquired gainful employment.

In later years, my mom also relocated to the city but had no way of supporting herself. She had little choice but to take in boarders to sustain herself and my two younger siblings, Stephanie and Larry. It was a very difficult time for them because my father was terminally ill and suffered a coronary thrombosis, from which he didn't survive. It was a very sorrowful time for our family.

Through her traditional and nontraditional culinary skills and relentless hard work, my mom developed a catering service. At the age of sixty-five, she suffered a stroke that disabled her until her death at the age of ninety-three.

After my mother's stroke, my then husband and I took over the catering service. With diligence and also hard work at our two full-time jobs during the week, my husband and I were able to acquire our beautiful acreage in Sherwood Park, which I highlighted previously. That home was so special to us, filled with fond memories of having lived there with our children. I still miss it.

I want to backtrack now to my drowning experience at the age of seventeen. On one occasion, my mother, one of my girlfriends, and I decided to have a vacation at Sylvan Lake. On a cool Wednesday morning, my friend and I ventured out to wade in the lake. We stayed near the shore, but suddenly I dropped and was pulled down into a very deep dugout. I realized I was drowning. I desperately tried to call for help, but before I could utter the word, I was forcefully pulled down to the bottom of the lake about three times. I thought I could crawl along the bottom of the lake back to the shore, but I was vigorously pulled up and down, again and again.

At that time, I was engaged to be married to Ed. As I was drowning, a vision flashed before me of myself in a beautiful white wedding gown. Then I was pulled down again. (Ed and I never married; I was too young. I learned many years later that he and a friend had drowned in a lake while fishing when their boat capsized. Ed's body wasn't recovered until six months later. He was a very kind and compassionate person. He was and always will be missed by many.)

The area around the lake was deserted, but fortunately for me, a young man was there repairing his boat, the only other person on the lake. He heard my calls for help and pulled me to safety. I couldn't reach him later to thank him, but I recall that his name was either Peter Tindale or Tisdale. My friend didn't wade into the dugout, so she was safe. I learned later that this huge dugout, about twelve feet deep, was for a tour boat that transported passengers around the lake. They were on a tour that morning.

On another occasion, I was in a car that rolled three times in a ditch on a country roadside. The driver apparently had consumed alcohol, was driving carelessly, and had lost control of the vehicle. I hit the dashboard, and several of my teeth were dislodged and broken. The other passenger suffered a broken collarbone. The driver was unhurt. We were traveling to a dance at Lakeview Pavilion. I loved dancing and still do. I was lucky again to have survived another incident.

The intervening years from 1954 to 1989 were not uneventful, but they were fulfilling and rewarding. The highlight of my life has undoubtedly been my part in raising Ernie's and my wonderful children, Sherry Leah, Carey Ernest, and Cory Jayson.

Letters to My Children

On a recent Labour Day weekend in September, 2017, through loneliness, I was happy to schedule a visit to Southgate Shopping Centre. This I arranged through DATS Van, accompanied by my wheelchair. DATS is a disabled adult transport service, which I hadn't been able to successfully travel in during the past.

I enjoyed being at the mall, especially as I had no flashbacks. While there I purchased a memoir at Coles Book Store entitled: Finding Me, by Michelle Knight. A very profound and heartbreaking story. I love reading memoirs.

While reading this memoir, although of entirely differing circumstances, I was taken by the author's captivating anecdotes of her love for her son, Joey. It brought to mind, as it often does, of just how special my own children are to me and perhaps I was too attached to them. I recalled the letters I had written to my children after leaving my marriage and my acreage home in Sherwood Park in 1998. These letters I kept in a safe place and, as yet, I have not delivered them to my children.

When I wrote these letters I lived in McDonald Place, a high rise apartment on the top floor (I could only afford to live there for a few months.) But I enjoyed the scenic view of the river valley.

When I could I would take long walks, passing the Shaw Conference Centre, where I would go into their restrooms for a drink of water or to wash my hands. I could continue on crossing a bridge over the river which led to Mill Creek Ravine. I don't recall having any friends at the time and these excursions were truly the highlight of my stay at McDonald Place. I—unfortunately, continued to have health issues related to PTSD, hallucinations, depression, and loneliness, with some bizarre actions on my part. But I was able to paint and write these letters.

After rereading them almost two decades later, they confirm explicitly my affectionate feelings for my children, and now their loved ones. Perhaps perceived by some as too emotional; I have nonetheless decided to disclose them in my memoir.

Dearest Sherry Leah:

Where to I begin to tell you how precious and special you are to me and to others, I know. Truly, one of the happiest days of my life was September 12, 1964, the day you made your debut into this wonderful world we live in. I can't tell you too often how much joy you brought into our family and still do in many wonderful ways. I reflect on the day you were born—So!. beautiful. Lots of dark hair and that endearing smile radiating even then, your profound beauty.

Our first born—we took you along everywhere we went. I had this baby seat that I'd place on the counter when I worked in the kitchen and you entertained me with those radiant smiles and the joy in your eyes. Your daddy would come home on his lunch breaks just to see you—how you were loved and still are.

One of the saddest days was when you were 3 and one-half months old and I took a job at the Provincial Lab. My heart ached at work—*I missed you so. But we were fortunate in that aunty Kaye looked after you lovingly and you bonded strongly with her. I'm happy about that but regret not having been with you at home longer. You were such an angel—charming, spirited, not demanding, and, all too soon, you grew into a delightful little lady.*

When Carey and Cory came along you were so motherly, never complaining about perhaps needing more attention. When I worked evenings at the Cancer Clinic we would leave each other notes and I couldn't wait to get home to read them. You thought I was a bit of a tiger?! Still am! Sometimes!

But this is a letter about love and all you mean to me. Perhaps, if not now, one day it may become more meaningful to you. I watched you grow, saw your hurts and hurt along with you—for you. You had many successes and were modest about them—have not known you to brag. Not when you were Carnival Queen at Terrace Heights, your numerous baton accomplishments, as well as then a Cheerleader, then we moved to Sherwood Park; your successful accomplishments in piano. Are you ready for it now? Will you play it?

I appreciate that you are close with Carey and Cory. I never see or hear envy only concerns and support for one another. I'm delighted that you can keep it that way and hope it never changes. Please don't shield me from any mishaps or misfortunes, if I were allowed to know if and when there is misfortune, I'd be stronger, better and helpful. I often feel I am not now what I'd like to be and think I was a caring mother, but not without faults.

Perhaps a sound analogy would be to address our weaknesses and try and turn them into strengths. I would like that and there must be good logical reasons for disbarring me from events that most families' share and discuss conjointly. One must know when to step aside and even accept rejection but that won't stop me from loving you, more than you can really imagine, worrying about you and living to hear from you. Some instincts are so profound - some right, I'm sure, some bizarre, and comes the need for bilateral communications. But I cannot force myself on you and apologize that I call so often and pray to hear you tell me about your day, your life, if you wish; but instead I just carry on and on while you listen. I must learn to wait for your call instead and have faith that you are well, safe, loved and protected!

I can't quite understand why I feel you are under stress but can't or won't share it. If you only knew that I wish to do everything to help, not hinder you, to the point of being a nuisance.

How did I get to here when this is supposed to be all about love. I cherish the years you and your brothers were growing up; our motor home vacations at Mara Lake and Penticton - floating on air mattresses, going to the Island, shucking oysters, digging for clams, fishing etc. I hope that you too have some good memories of "The Way We Were"—Good Times.

I regret that you children have to experience the trauma of your father's and my marriage break-up, and I appreciate that you have strong loving relationships with your dad; makes me feel that if you were in need of anything that you would go to him, if not to me. In time when my own pain and hurt heals, things will be different and meetings will be more controlled, if and when they occur.

Truly, in spite of all that has transpired, the finale is still the greatest shock of my life—one I will take to my grave and shocks me that it appears to be so insignificant. But I am progressing comfortably, albeit painfully, with no psychiatric labels only unresolved hurt and lack of dual communication when needed. Time heals many wounds for all of us.

But, back to you. I wish I could hear more about your job, perhaps meet you for lunch, but understand that your work must exhaust you and you need your rest.

If you need any help in any way, please ask. You never do. You know when you were in Australia, I lived for those letters you'd write, always updating us on what you were doing with assurance that there was never any need to worry. I'm glad you had that experience and to Europe too - perhaps Bermuda may not have been long enough - but you've seen much of the world and have many cherished memories.

Love is still the strong factor here and everyone needs that. I'll try not to impose too much, and thanks for letting me spend a couple of nights there. I'm OK now—getting braver and feeling safer. I wish that you and everyone shared that confidence.

Just need to tell you again that you mean the world to me (appended: As do the loved ones of *Your Lives.*)

I'll never stop loving you with all my heart and soul. The universe couldn't have been complete without Carey, Cory and you, and Stu in it., including: (Appended March 14, 2009, With Deepest Love to Walker and Carson.)

Love Forever and Ever,

Mom

Letter to Carey Ernest (verbatim)

August 20, 1999 (32nd Birthday)

Dearest Carey Ernest:

Where and how do I begin to tell you how special you are to me, now and always!

August 20, 1967, was one of the happiest days of my life when you made your debut into this beautiful world and into our lives, our family.

I cherish every precious memory of your growing years, and as I look at you today, you still have so many of those wonderful qualities that you had even as a very young child. You give of yourself so freely and never ask for anything. The other night I observed how you offered Cory a glass of water first, before you had any. You do special things for me and you seem to know what is required without being asked. You had an instinct you were needed and came out twice in the midst of my move, always helping.

I have been truly blessed with having you, Sherry and Cory. The three of you have been so good, never causing us, your parents, any worry. Often I got the instinct that you too might need help or are troubled and all I can do is phone—but you never complain. I should take a lesson from you.

When you were aged 2 and one-half and were already ill we were so grateful that all worked so positively and you survived. The bond established with you is so profoundly deep— *I feel it and when I look into your eyes it's as if I could look into your soul. (Addendum: After you had recovered you said: "I'm Lures Mom.")*

I pray with all my heart that you will be blessed with a long, happy and healthy life filled with love; given and received. May your career flourish, your personal relationships be strongly bonded, with love and God's blessings. Please nurture yourself as you do others!

I regret that you must witness the ugliness that has come about as a result of your parents break-up. I wish I could have handled it better and not have you witness what I was feeling and experiencing, but what transpired was truly the last thing I expected. Forgive me for where I have failed you because of my personal trauma. I will endeavor to be the best that I can be, and believe me I do and have tried. It feels awful to fail—when someone you once loved and trusted goes totally against everything you are and do—the challenge to survive is so totally immense. I hope you can understand. It's understood that children care for both parents and I promise to refrain from thinking we are still a family unit. I must and will stay out of the way—incidents that continually cut deeper.

That is not why I am writing this letter. I'd written one to Sherry and will be doing so to Cory soon too. I just feel that too often the loving words go unspoken, the endearing qualities go unaddressed, and you have so many wonderful qualities; I needed to tell you that. I often wonder what life would be like if I didn't have the three of you—whom I love and cherish as I do the loved ones of *Your Lives.*

I can't thank you enough for understanding where I'm at and forgiving when I blunder. I will always love you, respect you, and if you need anything that I can help you with, please ask. I'd never knowingly fail you.

Wishing you the happiest of birthdays and thoughts will be with you until we meet again.

Thank you for Everything you do.

With My Love Always,

Mom

Letter to Cory Jayson (Verbatim)

August 24, 1999

Dearest Cory Jayson:

Where do I begin to tell you how special and precious you are to me—and to many others, I know.

Another one of the happiest days of my life was January 18, 1971, when you made your debut into this world. A time when we were living in the country—free of war, beautiful and prosperous. Our family could never have been complete without you! I'll even go a step further to say the whole universe could not have been complete without you in it!

It is wonderful to have the mother's privilege of boasting with some exhilaration, to the right person, telling him how much he means to her: You! Your uniqueness and comprehension sometimes astounds me. You are clearly adept in what you say and do, and often do what is required without saying. You are appreciated for all you are—your goodness.

So loving and adorable, quite a perfectionist in so many ways, but with good reason. The place setting at the table had to be set just right, and often we were too busy. This didn't stop you. At the age of 9 or 10 you were already able to give me a shopping list of what was required to make egg rolls and other Chinese specialties. You had a culinary interest even then and have come to be quite the gourmet cook, who puts me to shame. And you have patience doing it. I miss all those pizzas you used to turn out—with great patience.

When you were small you had gotten into some meds and I had to rush you to the hospital with only a diaper on and bare footed. You were and are such a joy to have around. When you were very young you suffered a lot of pain and distress with your gastric system and often we didn't understand your pain, your agony, and tears.

In kindergarten you sang like a bird and loved it. Grade one was a bit rough and I'm sad about that but it's a known fact that intelligent persons see things a different way and you do, with clarity. You're analytical and base your decisions on sound judgment.

And when you were very young you very methodically made out a budget for our summer vacation in the motor home we once had. I hope you have some pleasant memories of the lake in Penticton, for instance, or the Island - cooking oysters which you called chicken; digging for clams.

Do you remember the fishing trip in Tofino where a fish hook caught your eyelid and luckily missed your eye. Remember how Sherry, Carey, you and I would float around on the air mattresses on the lake, build sand castles, and your dad would barbecue. But you grew older and so did we and nothing stays the same.

Very grateful to have Sherry, Carey and you. It warms my heart that you get along, care for, and love one another. If the words are hard to say sometimes, that's OK, because you feel it deep within you—as I do when I look into your eyes.

Do you remember the fall off the motorcycle and how Sherry looked after you and protected you. Let's try and do that now because I'm not sure exactly why she is stressed out and I can't seem to be able to help her. I'm glad the three of you are there for each other—because often I feel I may get in the way; but just so you know that's because I love each of you so, and would do anything to help if only you would ask. You have given us no trouble and never ask for anything. I wished so much that the acreage could go to the three of you—that was my dream!

I love the endearing cards you send me - always so thoughtful. Strange that I'm the parent yet I often go to each of you for reassurance and guidance. Should be reversed.

I am truly sorry that we are no longer a complete family. In all honesty, it was the last thing I expected, in spite of the hurdles. I do appreciate that you care and need to be with both parents and, in time, my own anger will subside and things will get better, I hope.

There is so much that is so good, and as I said on our 25th wedding anniversary: "I love being your mom." I'm impressed with your allegiance to Sammy. I wish that anything you are longing for will come your way and I am still waiting to hear your music. Maybe one day you will make a little tape so I can play it on my recorder.

I hope you will have a wonderful holiday, albeit short; it's nice that Carey will have a few days to spend with you. And when you return I hope that your work-load decreases.

I'm also recalling how you composed your own music at around grade 4, and did a piano recital at a school concert. I wish I'd have bought you a violin—I think you really wanted one. Is it too late now?

I hope and pray with all my heart and soul that you will have true love, good health, a prosperous career, and at least some of the joy that you give to me. I often wonder what life would be like without the three of you—whom I love and cherish (and addendum: "As I do the loved ones of *Your Lives.*"

Love You Always,

Mom

Leonora (also known as Leona) was born in the country near Andrew, Alberta, Canada. Times were difficult....so at the age of 16 she relocated to Edmonton, Alberta, where she furthered her education at Alberta and McTavish Colleges. She was employed as a medical dicta-transcriptionist, primarily within the medical milieu with and for some of the best, in spite of her profound hearing loss.

In the prime of her life, this all ended abruptly, when she was struck down by a transport vehicle and became a victim of post-traumatic stress disorder (PTSD). In addition to her failing health issues, physically and psychologically, this put an end to her working career, followed by the loss of a beautiful country estate, and ultimately—"her marriage." The effects of the accident and losses prevailed, but she didn't give-up.

Being a lover of nature, she enrolled in an Art Class, creating almost 100 oil and watercolor scenic paintings in ala prima technique......with perseverance and some highly qualified instruction. Although she struggled with frequent spasmodic attacks, these were subdued while she was distracted by and engrossed in her Art Work....."It was a form of therapy for her and helped her heal from trauma, a little."

Leona became an enthusiastic artist, and has previously been a member of the Art Society of Strathcona County and subsequently the Art Gallery of Alberta, where she has shown some of her work. Due to a mobility problem requiring the use of a wheel chair at most times, she has been able to exhibit her work only minimally.

Leonora finds solace being in the country—"*close to nature*"— also being an ardent spectator of Art, in any medium or format, by some talented artists. She revels in the literacy of good literature, and is enraptured by some of the outstanding musical compositions, when she doesn't have an auditory malfunction. She finds great comfort in some endearing comradeships, especially that of her grandsons, *Walker and Carson*, fortified by the embellishing love of her family. Leona and her husband, Ernie, who was deceased in 2013, have three children*: Sherry, Carey and Cory*.

Leona lives in Edmonton, Alberta, Canada.

Printed in the United States
By Bookmasters